The Royal Armouries in Leeds

The making of a museum

The Royal Armouries in Leeds

The making of a museum

DEREK WALKER

GUY WILSON

ACKNOWLEDGEMENTS

Front cover
The Yorkshire Electricity Hall of Steel: a detail from a painting of the Royal Armouries Museum by Carl Laubin
Inside covers
Computer-generated artwork for the displays in the Hall of Steel
Frontispiece
Armour for the joust of war from the court of the Emperor Maximilian I, German, about 1500
Illustrated material
Courtesy of AVE, Buro Happold, Elizabeth Bury, Derek Walker Associates, Goppion, Reflex Interactive, Imperial War Museum, Minale Tattersfield, National Portrait Gallery, Royal Armouries, The Works
Photographers
Principal photographers were Richard Davies and Jeremy Hall; other photographs supplied by Nobby Clark, Gordon Goode, Ken Kirkwood, Thom Richardson, Jan Walker, Samantha Lawrence Walker, Paul White, York Press Agency
Drawings and paintings
Julian Baker, Elizabeth Bury, Ric Duffield, Gerry Embleton, Markus Geiger, Carl Laubin, Aaron McCaffrey, Neil Miller-Chalk, David Reddick, Michael Ridden, Brian Tattersfield, Mary Tattersfield, Jane Tattersfield, Derek Walker, John Wright

Royal Armouries Museum
Armouries Drive
Leeds LS10 1LT

First published 1996

ISBN 0 948092 26 2

Printed in Great Britain.

Contents

TOURNAMENT
WAR

TOURNAMENT

Introduction

LORD EDEN OF WINTON

In 1986 when I was appointed Chairman of the Royal Armouries, the search for a new museum was already under way. The need for extra space was compelling. Only about 10% of the superb collection of arms and armour was on public display; the rest was either in storage or on loan. Yet the 1983 National Heritage Act which established the museum in its present form, placed upon the Trustees the duty publicly to display the collection; and to promote the public enjoyment and understanding of arms and armour.

That could not be achieved within the restricted confines of the Tower of London – the historical home of the Royal Armouries. So the decision was taken to move the greater part of the collection to a new site out of London. This would make possible major new displays of those items remaining in the Tower, as well as providing visitors to the Tower with improved facilities and better value for money. In 1991, having explored many alternatives, the Board of Trustees with the Secretary of State's agreement, finally decided in favour of Leeds. By Christmas of 1993 all the funding and legal agreements were in place and early in 1994 work began on site.

Leeds proved to be an enlightened choice. The City Council, the Development Corporation, the business community and the University all combined in the most imaginative way in order to help the project go forward. The support of local MPs and of the press, television and radio has also been consistent and invaluable. From the outset Leeds opinion has been wholly positive, showing a clear understanding of the benefits that such a significant development would bring in terms of new jobs, new buildings, and heightened economic activity.

For the first time the United Kingdom now has a major national museum located outside London in a purpose-designed building. It is the first example in the arts of the Government's Private Finance Initiative. In this the Department of National Heritage, the investment consortium led by 3i, the Leeds Development Corporation and Leeds City Council have been the key participants. But the idea, the initiative and the inspiration for the project came from the Royal Armouries and the dedicated individuals working closely with them.

The lot of the pioneer is not always an easy one. It was inevitable that during the long years of gestation there would be setbacks and difficulties. That these were overcome and the forward momentum maintained is a tribute to the resolution and vision of the Trustees, the Master and his staff and the many specialist experts helping them.

The result of all their effort is this fine new museum. From now on one of the world's greatest collections of arms and armour will be housed in ideal conditions. Imaginative displays and the most advanced techniques will present the objects in their proper context, bringing history to life and providing educational and entertainment opportunities of the highest quality.

I have absolutely no doubt that visitors of all ages will be thrilled by what they see and learn. And that the Royal Armouries new museum will prove to be an outstanding success.

Above: Lord Eden of Winton.
Left: The opening of the museum by Her Majesty the Queen and the presentation of the royal masque, 15 March 1996.

The concept

GUY WILSON

History of the Royal Armouries
The Royal Armouries is Britain's oldest national museum, and one of the oldest museums in the world.

It began life as the main royal and national arsenal housed in the Tower of London. Indeed the Royal Armouries has occupied buildings within the Tower for making and storing arms, armour and military equipment for as long as the Tower itself has been in existence.

Although distinguished foreign visitors had been allowed to visit the Tower to inspect the Royal Armouries from the 15th century at least, at first they did so in the way a visiting statesman today might be taken to a military base in order to impress him with the power of the country. In the reign of Queen Elizabeth I less exalted foreign and domestic visitors were allowed to view the collections, which then consisted almost entirely of relatively recent arms and armour from the arsenal of King Henry VIII. To make room for the modern equipment required by a great Renaissance monarch Henry had cleared the Tower's stores of the collections of his medieval predecessors.

The Tower and its Armouries were not regularly opened to the paying public until King Charles II returned from exile in 1660. Visitors then came to see not only the Crown Jewels but also the 'Line of Kings', an exhibition of some of the grander armours, mounted on horses made by such sculptors as Grinling Gibbons and representing the 'good' Kings of England, and the 'Spanish Armoury', containing weapons and instruments of torture said to have been taken from the 'Invincible Armada' of 1588. The Royal Armouries had become, in effect, what it has remained ever since, the national museum of arms and armour.

During the great age of Empire-building which followed, the collections grew steadily. Until its abolition in 1855, the Board of Ordnance, with its headquarters in the Tower, designed and tested prototypes and organised the production of huge quantities of regulation arms of many sorts for the British armed forces. Considerable quantities of this material remain in the collections today, and some can be seen on the walls of the Hall of Steel. Also, throughout this period captured weapons continued to be sent to the Tower and displayed as proof of Britain's continuing military successes.

Early in the 19th century the nature and purpose of the museum began to change radically. Displays were gradually altered from exhibitions of curiosities to historically 'accurate' and logically organised displays designed to improve the visitor by illuminating the past. As part of this change items began to be added to the collection in new ways, by gift and purchase, and this increased rate of acquisition has continued to this day.

In this way the collection has developed enormously, the 'old Tower' material being joined in the last 150 years by the world-wide comparative material which now makes the Royal Armouries one of the greatest collections of its type in the world.

From 1977 onward, under the direction of the then Master of the Armouries, Nick Norman, the museum began to consider expanding

Above: Top, Brian Tattersfield's identity for the Royal Armouries in Leeds; centre, the grotesque helmet, presented by Maximilian I to Henry VIII, on which it is based; bottom, application of the visual identity in three dimensions.
Opposite: A selection of the arms and armour displayed by the Royal Armouries in the Tower of London before 1995, showing its scope and variety.

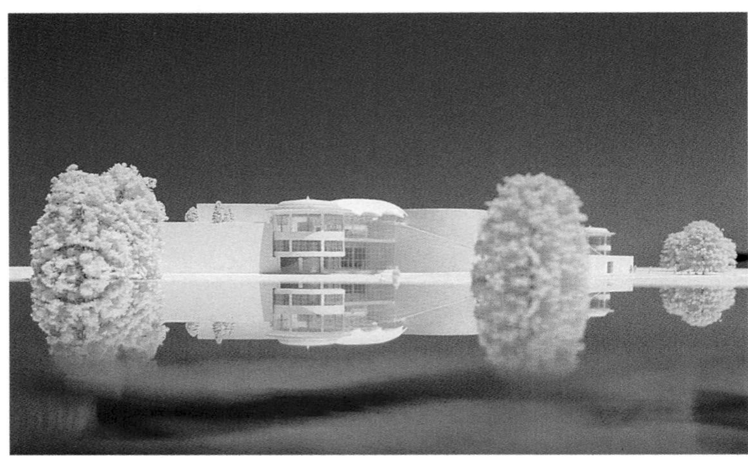

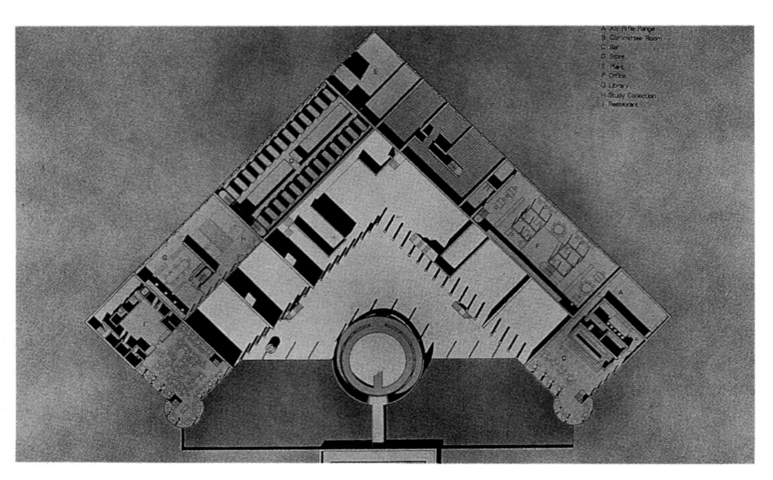
A Air Rifle Range
B Committee Room
C Bar
D Store
E Plant
F Office
G Library
H Study Collection
I Restaurant

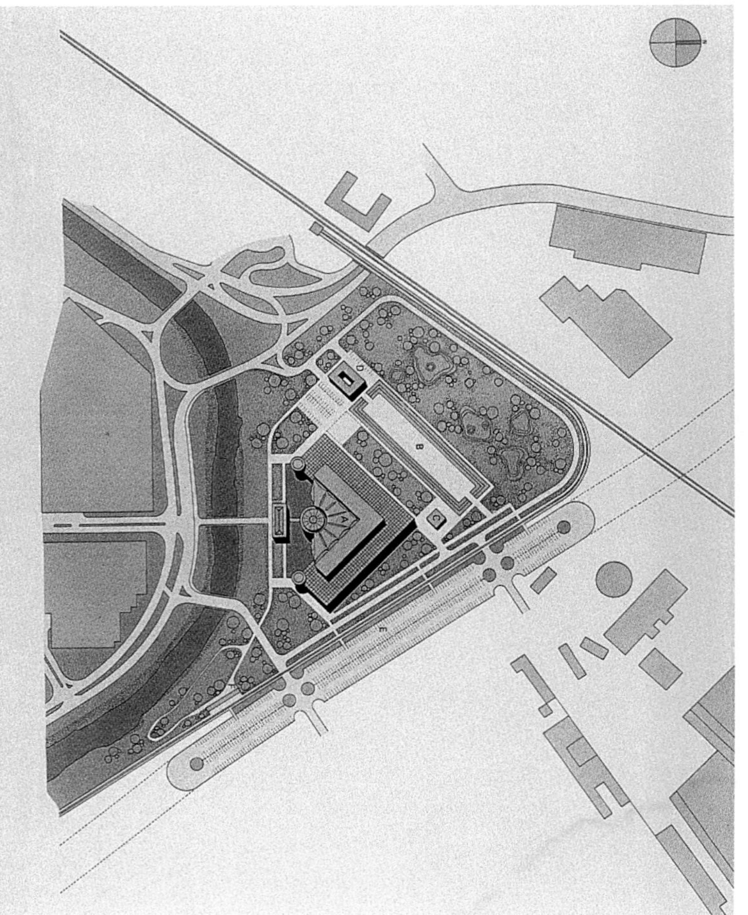

outside of the Tower to increase public access to its growing and increasingly diverse collections. Ten years later the Royal Armouries signed a lease with Hampshire County Council and took possession of Fort Nelson, near Portsmouth, which it now runs as a museum for its large collection of artillery. For the first time in its long history the Royal Armouries was responsible for displays outside of the Tower of London.

In the following year, 1988, we took a step back from the pressure of immediate work and began to consider the long-term future of the museum and its collection. We wanted to increase public access still further and give ourselves opportunities to show and interpret the major parts of the collection which had no direct relationship to the Tower of London outside of the restricting confines of an ancient royal palace and fortress run by another organisation.

In 1990, after two years of preliminary research and deliberation, the decision was taken to establish a new Royal Armouries in the north of England in which to house the bulk of the collection of world-wide arms and armour, thus allowing the Royal Armouries in the Tower to concentrate upon the display and interpretation of those parts of the collection which directly relate to the Tower of London. The concept of the Royal Armouries in Leeds had been born, although at this stage Leeds had not been selected.

Thereafter the development of the concept and the search for a location and the necessary funding went hand in hand. At first plans were drawn up and negotiations undertaken to site the new museum in Sheffield's Lower Don Valley. Then other cities expressed an interest and a short-list was drawn up from which the Trustees of the Armouries made their final selection. By 1991 Leeds had been chosen as the location. By 1992 funding of £28.5 m had been secured – £20 m from the Department of National Heritage, £5m from Leeds Development Corporation and £3.5 m from Leeds City Council – subject to the remaining £14 m required being raised from the private sector. Meanwhile the merchant bankers Schroder Wagg had been appointed as financial advisers to the Royal Armouries and had been working with the senior staff of the museum, the Department of National Heritage and its predecessor with responsibility for the Armouries, the Department of the Environment, and the Treasury to find a way of involving private-sector investment in the project. By the spring of 1993 an investment memorandum had been approved and the new museum was ready to be launched as the first Private Finance Initiative project in the heritage sector. The venture-capital company 3i quickly took up the challenge and by mid summer Sir James Glover had been appointed Chairman and Christopher O'Boyle Chief Executive of a nascent company, Royal Armouries International. By 14 December 1993 all investments and all agreements were in place and after five years of planning the new museum was certain of becoming a reality. All that has been achieved since has been done by the private and public sector partners working closely together. Both the partnership and the result are unique.

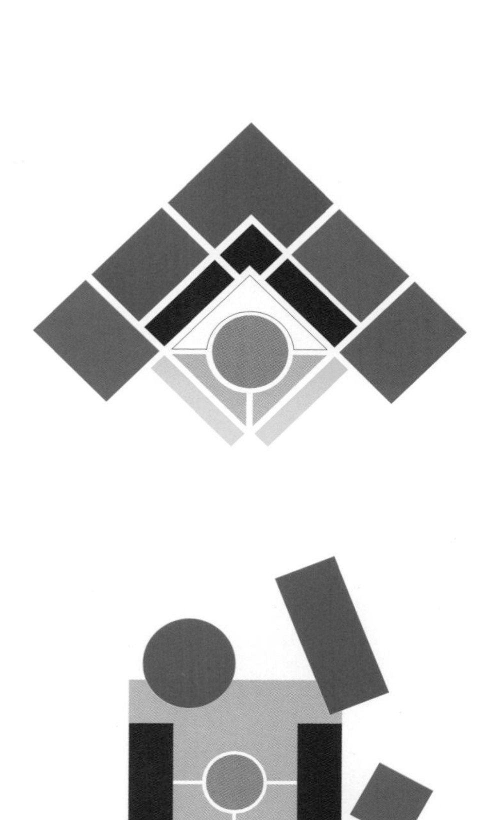

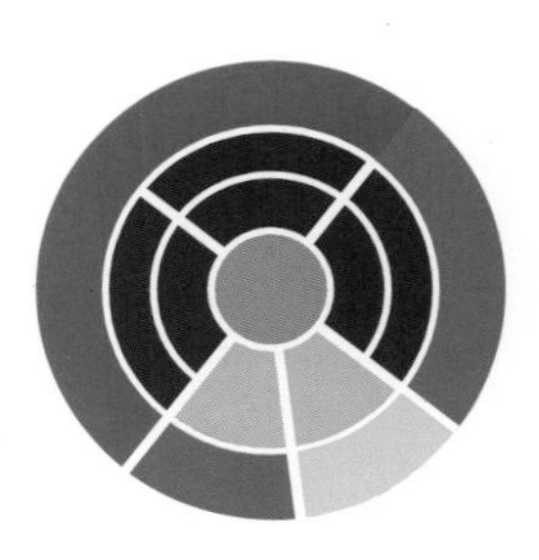

Above: Types of museum: concepts and floor plans used in the development of the proposed Royal Armouries site in Sheffield.
Opposite: Views of the model, site plan and ground-floor plan for the proposed Royal Armouries in Sheffield.

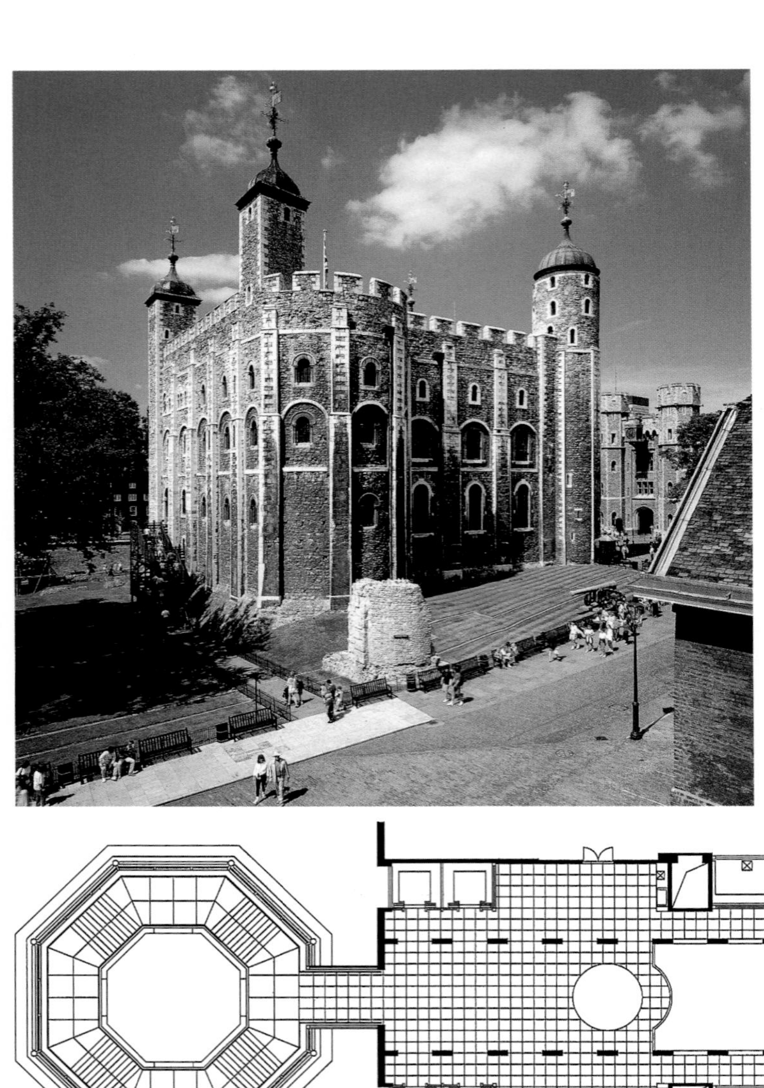

The new Royal Armouries

The new museum was developed specifically to show the collections of the Royal Armouries to the visiting public in the best possible way. Therefore we began with the question 'How do we want to display our collections?', and the answer to that, together with answers to questions about how the work of the museum was organised, has dictated the sort of building which we commissioned.

The answer came in two parts. First, we agreed that we wanted to tell the stories of the development and use of arms and armour around the world for war, sport, hunting, self-defence and fashion. Second, we decided that to do this successfully we needed to use all the available modern communication and exhibition techniques – including film and audio-visual aids, tableaux, hands-on opportunities to learn using both computers and real objects, and live demonstrations of craft and weapons-handling skills.

These decisions were used to develop a brief for the architectural and design teams which led them to develop the sort of museum building that we wanted. The original architectural brief was a long document but it is worth repeating the objectives with which it began for they have been the framework for the whole design process:

1. To create a building which properly houses and displays the collections of the museum.
2. To create a building capable of housing approximately 200 staff, and catering for up to 1.26 m visitors each year.
3. To create a friendly and welcoming building which reflects the quality and excitement of the collections and displays within.
4. To create a quality landmark building for the Clarence Dock site and for the whole of Leeds.
5. To create a building which can serve the local community, and which is capable of hosting a wide variety of evening functions, sometimes several at the same time.
6. To create a building with a long life, made of good, easily maintained materials.
7. To do all the above in the most cost effective manner within the current budget figure of £ 22 m.

Fundamentally in design terms there are only two sorts of museum: 'processional' museums in which the visitor is led from room to room in a particular order, usually chronological, sometimes thematic; and 'radiating' museums in which the visitor explores the displays from a central point in any order.

Given that we wanted to tell a series of linked but different stories, each of which could be enjoyed on its own, or in any order, the architectural brief asked for a 'radiating' museum with a central circulation spine from which the galleries could be visited in any sequence. From this and the overriding need to make the building welcoming and friendly the Street was born, a canyon-like atrium rising the full height of the museum from which every gallery is approached.

The Royal Armouries was not intended to be a 'black-box visitor attraction'; it has been designed as a museum for the 21st century using the best of traditional museum design, and it has been developed quite consciously to show its collections in relation to the real world in which we live. The displays seek to make the historical stories relevant by bringing

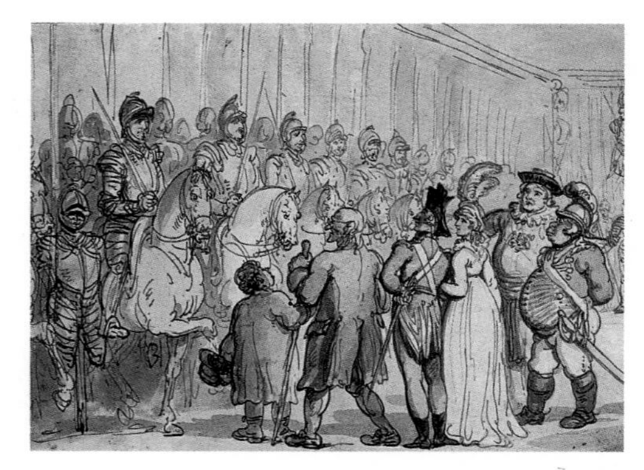

Above: Top, the Line of Kings in the Tower of London, pen-and-wash drawing by Thomas Rowlandson, about 1800; bottom, the Alexander mosaic in the Archaeological Museum, Naples.
Opposite: Top left, the White Tower at the Tower of London; top right, a 13" mortar battery at Fort Nelson; centre, a plan of the Street; bottom left, the Victoria Arcade in Leeds; bottom right, a model of the Clarence Dock master plan prepared by Derek Walker Associates for the Leeds Development Corporation.

them up to the present day. The building was designed to reinforce this by allowing the modern world to permeate into the galleries in which those stories are told.

The architectural brief made it clear that the museum's collections and the ideas of how best to display and interpret them would be paramount:

> The building is the vessel which contains the displays and allows them to succeed. Display must dominate every element, area, and floor of the museum. Even when not in the galleries the visitor must be made aware of the collections by sympathetic design and theming. The Royal Armouries is determined that its new museum will be designed properly so that it provides a fitting home for the collections of the museum. In order to achieve this, the needs of the collection and its display must dominate the design of the building.

The building has, quite literally, been designed around the collections of the museum, and the individual galleries within it have been arranged to allow the visitor to take in the experience. The displays are intended to entertain and stimulate a desire to learn without trivialising their subjects. This has meant developing a rhythm to the exhibitions so that there is a balance between standing and sitting, watching and doing, looking at real objects and explanatory films, reading text, static display and active demonstration, a balance which stimulates the desire to find out, and prevents aching feet and the yawn of boredom which all of us have experienced from time to time in museums.

One of the first creative documents produced during the development of the new museum was a paper on the concept of the displays. It stated:

> Every gallery incorporates an appropriate mix of display and communication techniques to explain and interpret the magnificent objects of the collection. This mix ranges from the traditional museum display of objects in cases to the live demonstration of the use of weapons and armour. The objects are set in a context by themed interior design, by guides and interpreters, and by film and other audio-visual aids. There is an emphasis on 'hands-on' learning, so that by contact with real or replica objects, and by interactive computer programmes, the visiting public can gain a real feeling for and understanding of the collections. The intention has been to create a multilayered experience to cater for the many different interests and interest levels of our visitors.

The new Royal Armouries has been designed to house the best collections of their type in the world and to allow them to be displayed and interpreted in a way which will inspire and inform the visitor. The pieces displayed range from the sumptuously ornamented armours and weapons of kings and courtiers of past centuries to the plain, functional, sometimes throw-away weapons of the modern soldier. All of them are displayed and interpreted as part of a story, or a series of stories, about how they were made and how they were used.

The use of violence by humankind for supremacy or survival, or its sublimation into sport or play, always has been, and probably always will be, one of the main forces for historical change. This is the underlying theme of the new Royal Armouries. It is a fascinating and disturbing story of great importance to us and our children. It is the responsibility of the new museum to make this story relevant for future generations.

Above: A cartoon published in 1827, entitled *The Wellington Boot or Head of the Army.*
Opposite: Models of the exterior and interior of the Yorkshire Electricity Hall of Steel; the first model of the entire building.
Following pages: Sectional perspective of the Yorkshire Electricity Hall of Steel; p.17, left, display and interpretation concepts and techniques which inspired the ideas for the new museum; right, films made for the Royal Armouries.

cycle
view
view rng
save
get
value
length
move
quit
flip
0 25
reset
value mode
copy
levels
select
current
extreme values, length:24
copy all
100 0
up
dn
0
1 frame
1
24
World
lights
wall
0.00 Stretch
0.00 UpArmRotz
0.000
0.00 UpArmRoty
0.000
11.430
0.00 UpArmRotz
0.000
-51.430
0.00 LoArmRotz
0.000
65.000

Choosing the design team

GUY WILSON

One design team covering all disciplines has worked on the project from the beginning, each member gaining inspiration from the others and at the same time contributing to their work. It is the first time in this country that every aspect of a museum has been designed from the beginning in this way.

This had always been the intention – those of us who developed the concept knew that we needed an integrated team to produce the seamless result to which we all aspired. The original architectural brief set the tone for the selection process:

> The visit to the museum must be a pleasurable, exciting, holistic and seamless experience, with innovative displays blending into the architecture developed to surround and enhance them. To achieve this the architect must work as part of a single creative team with the other consultants under the direction of the Master of the Armouries. The museum experience revolves around the displays and therefore the display design consultants will take the lead, working closely with the architect, on matters of interior and spatial design which will flow automatically from the needs of the displays and the related questions of visitor circulation and access. The display design team will also lead the development of the external event areas.

After a number of false starts in a complex learning process the need for close integration was solved by the appointment of the architect, Derek Walker, as the head of the display design team as well.

The project has been fortunate to have had the continuity of Derek Walker's involvement from the beginning. He worked on the design of the abortive Royal Armouries Museum in Sheffield, and all involved learnt much from the experience about what we wanted and how we could achieve it. As a result of this work his practice, Derek Walker Associates, was appointed by Leeds Development Corporation to produce the master plan for Clarence Dock incorporating a footprint for the new Royal Armouries Museum in Leeds. Finally, Derek Walker was appointed architect for the new museum early in 1993.

To succeed, any complex design process must involve a small group of people working closely together inspired by common aims and mutual respect. The relationship between architect and client is crucial for the development of a good building, that between display designer and client equally crucial for the development of good exhibitions. As Master of the Armouries and creative director of the whole project I have worked closely with Derek Walker in both those areas. The partnership has been a productive and stimulating one. I found that Derek shared my belief that major new museums should be designed from the inside out, shared my commitment to quality, and shared my desire to present our collections in context using a mixture of traditional and innovative display and interpretative techniques.

Derek Walker Associates had a fine record of achievement in large-scale

Above: Top, Guy Wilson, Master of the Armouries; bottom, Professor Derek Walker.
Opposite: The Whitney Museum exhibition model by Derek Walker and Norman Foster.

Welcome to Britain

master planning, building design, interior planning, furniture design, animation and graphics, a combination of great importance for the project. Their recent work in designing a variety of leisure, arts and recreational buildings in Kowloon Park, Hong Kong, were of particular significance to us, and the extraordinary interactive park that they developed with Wonderworld plc for Corby.

To amplify the considerable experience of Derek Walker's own team, we looked for the best in the graphic design world and the best in theatre design, film and television to work together as a team of all talents.

Minale Tattersfield, widely regarded for many years as one of the best design companies in Europe, were appointed to produce the new museum's corporate identity. Led by Brian Tattersfield, their role has been much broader than simply corporate identity work. Brian has been responsible for the graphic content of much of the museum and has made his mark even on the design of the building itself.

Derek Walker also introduced to the team John and Elizabeth Bury, who have brought a theatrical sensitivity and know-how to the design process.

Yorkshire Television were an early and stalwart ally in the days before many thought that the dream could become a reality. They helped enormously to raise the profile and credibility of the project and secure the first ministerial backing for it without which progress could not have been made. Their subsidiary, Chevron Communications, won the contract to produce all the audio-visual programmes for the new museum. Yorkshire Television have a fine reputation for and record of producing excellent drama, current affairs and educational programmes, a combination of expertise ideally suited to the new museum. Chris Meehan, Marketing Director of Chevron has been with the project from the beginning, first as apparently our only fan and latterly as senior executive responsible for delivering one of the most creative elements of the whole project. His 'view from the outside' concludes this section.

No great building can be successfully designed without good and creative structural and mechanical engineers, and no project can be completed on time and in budget without excellent quantity surveyors. Against very strong competition Buro Happold were awarded the comprehensive engineering commission and since then have worked closely as a part of the design team on both building and displays. Their expertise in lightweight roofing was crucial in the design of the Craft Court and Tiltyard, and their willingness to adopt innovative solutions to building management and environmental control systems has proved invaluable in designing a museum safe for priceless collections. The Leeds firm Rex Procter and Partners completed the design team when they were appointed as quantity surveyors to the project. Their local knowledge and justified reputation for accurate forecasting have been an essential element in the work of the whole team.

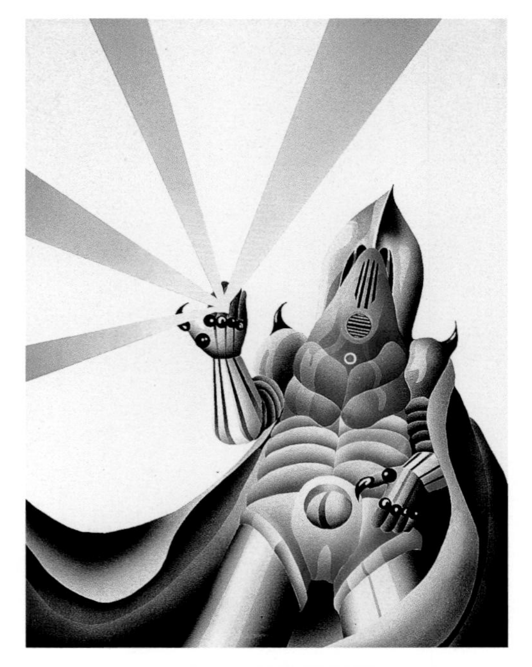

Above: Top, frame from an animated film of Wagner's *Ring*; bottom, model of Kowloon Park, Hong Kong. Both by Derek Walker Associates.
Opposite: Top left, Kowloon Park, Hong Kong; top right, Energy Pavilion, Wonderworld, both by Derek Walker Associates and Buro Happold; centre, sculpture park, Milton Keynes, by Derek Walker Associates; bottom left, poster by Minale Tattersfield for BAA; bottom right, timber lattice at Mannheim by Buro Happold.

A view from the outside

CHRIS MEEHAN

The invitation to meet Guy Wilson, the Master of the Armouries, and his team was irresistible. Come to the Yorkshire–Tyne-Tees studios to hear about the plans for the creation of a new museum and to share in the vision

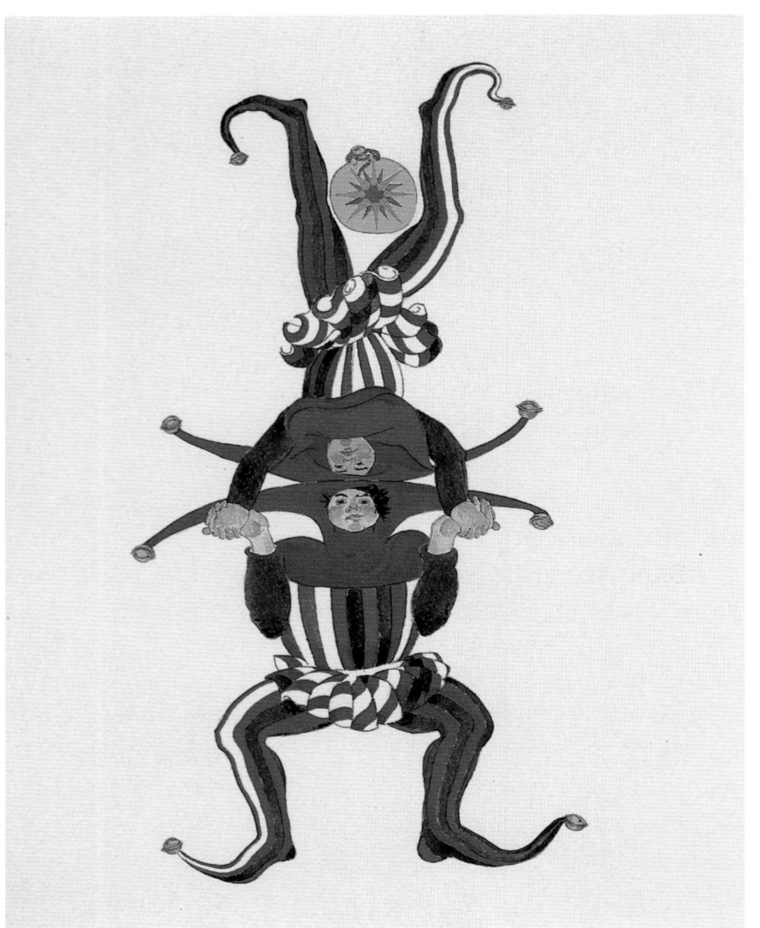

of 'a museum for the 21st century'.

It was early 1990, in a packed preview theatre at the Television Centre, that we first saw one man's vision for a new purpose-built Royal Armouries. His presentation, backed by imaginative visuals, was brought to life by his disarming, unstuffy and popularist approach to how museums should be. Not portentous and forbidding, but open, accessible, stimulating and exciting. He outlined a fantastic opportunity for the latest audio-visual techniques to complement the priceless collection of arms and armour on display and help tell the story of the development of weapons from earliest times. He went on to describe, as though he had been there, the scene at the battle of Agincourt and the likely thoughts of a hapless Frenchman, faced with upwards of 20,000 arrows raining down on his head, shot by the English longbowmen, in one of the most vivid examples of the effectiveness of medieval firepower. By the time he finished, I was elbowing my way forward to ask how I could get involved.

In the six years since then, through the many stages of development, through the often tortuous tendering process and the creation of the original design display team, through the many pitfalls, Wilson's vision never faltered.

Years spent travelling to speak to 'those that matter', presentations to the great and the good, business managers, potential investors, support groups, financiers and sponsors, took huge stamina. He made it fun and exciting for those around him. He knew, and because of that, we knew, that this was important work, that the vision would become reality, that it would succeed and that, therefore, no effort on its behalf was too great. Such was his desire to give the collections the home and presentation they deserved.

The task of interpreting the Wilson 'vision' fell to Derek Walker, the project architect and leader of the design display team, as well as the master planner for the site at Clarence Dock. A highly creative man with an enviable international reputation, he speaks his mind but he is also a great listener with a genuine regard for human relations. A team player prepared to hold out always for the best, Derek bound the creative team together with verve and tremendous flair, but both Wilson and Walker acknowledge a great debt to Lord Eden, the former Chairman of the Trustees who created the political will to make the move. The project owes much to him and many others, some, who, rather like rocket-boosters, blazed a trail in the early stages and then fell away, often through force of circumstance or simple human frailty. People such as Mike Harris, who sadly died before his time and before his film production skills could be fully utilised, but whose historical knowledge and sheer enthusiasm for the project moved and sustained the team throughout those early days. A mention too for David Wilson and Melanie Davis who, heroically, stepped into the breach and took over the reins of software production with tremendous diligence and great style and professionalism.

In January of 1996 Guy Wilson conducted a team of Royal Armouries' newly hired interpreters and a few old supporters on a tour of the new building. For him it was just another routine visit, for the rest of us it was a morning of significance. The 'vision' was at last almost a reality and a glorious one at that. To anyone reading his book who has not visited the new museum I say come and see it for yourself, and tell others to come and see for themselves. It is your and our heritage and a salutary lesson to all doubters that miracles occasionally happen.

Above: Top, Milton Keynes exhibition by Derek Walker and Brian Tattersfield 1971; bottom, Energy Pavilion, Wonderworld, by Derek Walker Associates and Buro Happold.
Opposite: Oberon from *A Midsummer Night's Dream,* set, costumes and lighting by John and Elizabeth Bury; right, targets for medieval shooting gallery by Mary Tattersfield.
Following pages: Painting of the museum by Carl Laubin.

VE 1995

SOPHIE
LUCY

CONSTRUCTION

The design process

DEREK WALKER

It is a rare privilege to be asked to design and realise a national museum together with its complex displays. It is even more satisfying to design it within the context of a master plan also prepared in one's own studio.

This privilege has been hard-earned; first, studying the collection in depth over a considerable period of time with Guy Wilson, the Master of the Armouries, second, being crucially involved in the preparation of the museum brief, leading to our abortive study for a site in Sheffield, which examined in three dimensions the possibility of designing a building in response to the collection; and third, winning the planning competition for Clarence Dock which gave us the opportunity to refine the brief, choose the ideal location for the museum and establish a provisional footprint for the building which has proved surprisingly robust.

Following the successful presentation of the master plan for Clarence Dock we were, in the face of stiff competition, awarded responsibility for the design of the displays in the new museum and after some debate the Trustees felt that the nature of their requirements so inextricably linked the display and the building that the most workable solution was to have one designer take on the combined commission.

Clarence Dock was constructed in the 1840s under the supervision of the engineer George Lether. It was made of giant gritstone blocks from the Pennines initially as a single 100 m x 50 m basin, but before the turn of the century extensions had been added to the west and south. The docks marked the head of the Aire and Calder Navigation which linked Leeds to Hull and the North Sea and enabled freight to be transferred to the smaller craft that could use the Leeds-Liverpool canal which linked the City with the Irish Sea and thence the Atlantic. Until its business was undermined by the railways Clarence Dock handled significant tonnages of mixed cargo, particularly timber and potatoes, in both transit and storage. In the early 20th century much of the land around the dock came to be used for recreation and sports, including both cricket and football, but over the years the area took on the characteristics of many waterside properties in the care of the British Waterways Board which had once had an important role linked to water-borne trade and the canal system but whose commercial importance had declined. There were sawmills and timber yards, oil and petrol storage depots, builder's merchant's yards and a lead-smelting plant. Debris and silt accumulated in the dock and water quality in both the river and the dock declined.

Nevertheless, this was by far the most promising of the five sites offered by competing cities when the decision was taken in 1991 to move a large part of the Royal Armouries collection from the Tower of London, its historical home, to the north of England. In addition to the stillness of the dock and the quiet drama of the river and weir the site offered a substantial catchment population and proximity not only to the city centre but also to the major motorways approaching the city from the south.

Above: Japanese garden detail, Kyoto.
Opposite: The Hall of Steel at night.

But the site was a difficult one in some respects, as became clear following agreement in 1992 on the release of a 14-acre tract for the Royal Armouries development.

The debate over the siting and massing of the building had to recognise that access for delivery vehicles was effectively confined to the south and east, where the main public entrance would also need to be, and by far the best site for construction, closest to the city centre and contained by the river and the dock, was bisected by a long-established road, Clarence Road, which bridged the entrance to the dock.

The solution was to secure agreement on the closure of Clarence Road thus creating a single open promontory between dock and river. Here the museum could have two waterfront elevations. The western stub of Clarence Road could be combined with the riverside towpath to provide pedestrian-only access from the city centre to the north. All vehicles could approach the building from the south and east via a simple one-way loop road tied back to Hunslet Road and the remains of Clarence Road.

This was a controversial decision. Clarence Road was a well-known, if not heavily used, route in Leeds and contained numerous main service cables, all of which had to be expensively diverted. But the decision was the right one. To have preserved Clarence Road and placed the building further south would have eroded its links with the city centre, destroyed its relationship with the main dock basin and created unusable parcels to the west and east of Clarence Road.

The disposition of the main elements of the building seemed to follow logically once this key decision had been taken. It was decided to limit deliberately the area available for construction by positioning the building as close as possible to the water edges, stacking the main galleries and supporting areas on six levels to complement Roberts Mart and Rose Wharf, two handsome, listed, 19th-century flax mills on the river's east bank which were both in the process of being recycled into new uses. This established the museum as the dominant and pivotal presence within the area, while providing enticing views of the city and surrounding hills from higher floors. The Tiltyard and its supporting facilities, the Craft Court and Menagerie Court, were laid out along the river bank east of the main building, and visitor parking was provided in the area south of the museum contained by the loop road.

These early decisions on positioning and massing provided a clear framework for the articulation of the main elements of the museum building itself. With its five main galleries vertically superimposed the building needed a single dramatic interior space to double as an entrance concourse and a consistent point of reference. The covered Street, some 54 m in length, rises 30 m through the full height of the building providing light penetration and a focus for front-of-house and out-of-hours activities at ground level. Located at the north end of the Street are the main lifts and Hall of Steel, a grand stairway containing a mass display of weapons and armour from the collection. At night the Hall of Steel with its internal lighting and glass lantern acts as a beacon to the city centre and is visible to traffic dipping over the crest of the hills on the M1 approach to the city from the south.

The Street is the link between the museum's main entrances from the dockside to the west and from the main drop-off and parking areas to the south. Around the Street the main elements of the museum are clearly

Above: Top, detail of a figure of a British Vickers machine-gunner of World War I in the War gallery; bottom, Maxim-Nordenfeldt machine gun of 1895 in the War gallery.
Opposite: View of the museum from the river.

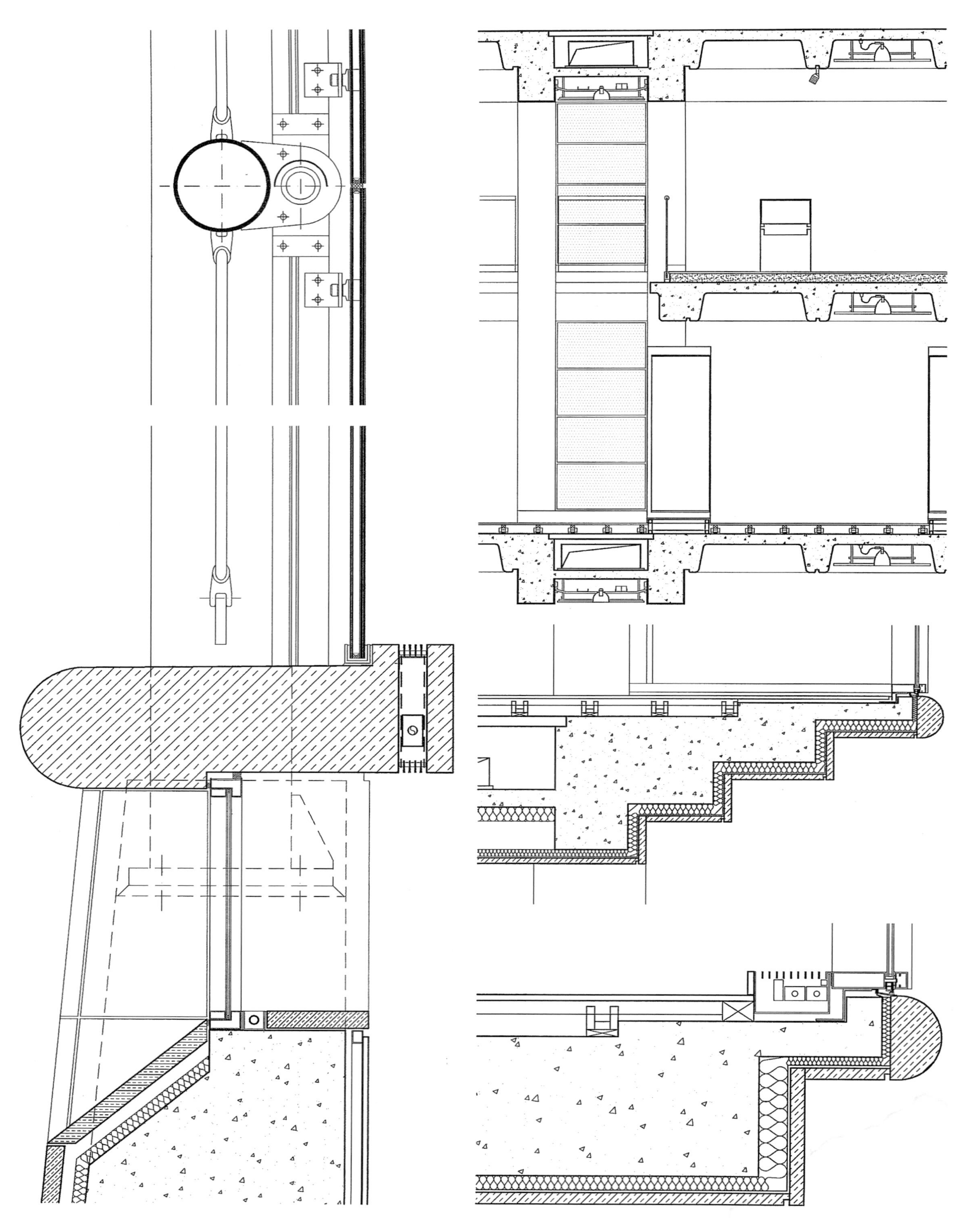

articulated; larger gallery spaces, cinema stack, Education Department and Library to the east, smaller gallery spaces, restaurants and shop to the west. Galleries are linked by bridges crossing the street at four levels. An administration block and storage/conservation block are at the south-east and south-west corners of the building where secured access for vehicles is integrated within the building envelope.

If the general arrangement of the building follows a logical interpretation of the client's needs, the spirit and fabric of the building is more difficult to place.

The preamble to Arthur Wise's book *The history and art of personal combat* haunted my thoughts throughout design development as it generated the crucial question of how to design a building dedicated to expose and present man's inhumanity to man and other animals.

> Violence has been an inescapable fact of human life since the beginning of time. It has been the ultimate arbiter of all conflicts between individuals and between nations. In a very real sense the history of violence is the history of humanity. Man is a violent animal with a veneer of civilised behaviour just covering the surface. It is not surprising that through the years he has given a great deal of thought to the most efficient ways of inflicting physical damage on his kind.

In reality this perceptive reflection contributed to our design approach which has attempted to invest the cool exterior of the building with an element of danger and menace in contrast to the colourful masque and festival trappings of its warm and welcoming interior persona; a building reflecting the paradox and ambiguity of the emotions the subject invites. To reflect these emotions we attempted to design a setting of high drama, easy to navigate and understand, rather like those Scottish castle plans so highly rated by Louis Kahn: a building with massive structural presence to achieve the demanding environmental conditions required for the display of the collection.

The materials of the exterior were chosen to reflect the character and quality of the collection – metallic engineering brick in gunmetal grey, stainless steel, bead-blasted and polished, and a mica-flecked pre-cast stone, all set on a generously coursed strong granite base. The oriels and great window walls, overlooking the river, park and docks, provide transparent viewing towers which complement the defensive nature of the enclosures to the galleries and storage areas. Mullions are powder-coated steel and aluminium in light grey, and a dark grey coating is used for all the gridded metalwork for the doors, gates, service entrances and individual balconies to the offices.

To encourage people to use the building the museum was designed to be open and permeable at ground level with free public access to the street, bistro, restaurant and museum shop. These spaces are fully glazed to both the Street and the Dock. The amount of glazing is reduced at the upper levels because of the need to ensure the security and physical preservation of the collections and to show them in dramatic settings requiring controlled rather than natural lighting. Nevertheless the importance of relating the collections and visitors to their surroundings has been recognised in the detailed design development and there are naturally lit areas in all the galleries where views of the river, Dock and park can be enjoyed while browsing through the collection, enjoying some refreshment or simply resting.

Above: Development sketches for the Edwardian gun room in the Hunting gallery (top) and the Indian gate in the Oriental gallery (bottom).
Opposite: Left, detail of the structure and servicing of the Hall of Steel; top right, typical gallery section; middle and bottom right, structure of the oriel windows.

The new Royal Armouries is intended to tell a series of stories about how arms and armour have been used through the ages. All of these stories are self-contained and can be visited and appreciated in any order. Because of this the museum has been designed with a simple central circulation pattern focused on the north end of the Street with the main displays located on the two upper floors, both part mezzanined. Each gallery is entered from the Street, which acts as a point of reference to prevent visitors from feeling disorientated or lost. Normal access between the different floors is by staircases or a battery of glazed lifts which allow the disabled the same free movement around the building as all other visitors.

The effect of this arrangement of the museum in three double-height storeys is to give the building a commanding presence in Clarence Dock. This is further enhanced by making a major feature of the main staircase at the end of the Street. This is contained in the Hall of Steel, a lofty octagonal tower, fully glazed above a two-storey granite podium. The generous staircase spirals up between the glazed outer wall and the solid inner octagon which rises from eight two-storey columns and provides on both sides of the octagon backing for mass wall displays of over 3,000 pieces of arms and armour at a level of density and complexity unseen in this country since late Victorian times.

The Royal Armouries exists to gather and preserve a collection and to use it to stimulate and educate. This duty to educate and inspire cannot be achieved simply by traditional display techniques. It is now widely accepted in the museum and teaching professions that objects from the past need to be explained and put in context if they are to be understood. The basic questions of who made them and how and who used them and why need to be answered. Objects made for use rather than purely for decoration must be seen in action if they are to be fully understood. All this needs to be done to stimulate and educate without oversimplifying and risking trivialisation.

One of my heroes, Sir Ernst Gombrich, made it clear in his discourse to a conference sponsored by the British Museum and American Assembly in 1975:

> Any window dresser, if I may put it so bluntly, can place an isolated Greek vase under a spotlight in an empty room and force it on our attention. The problem of showing a large collection of superficially similar objects rather than hiding most of them from view is of a different order of complexity. Perceptually it arises from the process of scanning and grouping. Arrange a class of objects in some simple geometrical order and you will find that it is the similarities which tend to stand out and even fuse like images in a kaleidoscope. Somehow we must make the visitor see the similarities but notice the differences. We have to find suitable means of visual emphasis and articulation guiding the scanning eye to focus on the most rewarding points but allowing it to linger anywhere. It is a task which cannot be left to the designer unless he consults at every step with the keeper who knows every piece intimately and has a coherent picture of the whole field. The result of this collaboration should be an arrangement which is intended to last at least as long as the vision of the past on which it is based.

I hope that the presentations in the new Royal Armouries represent this view, aided I trust by the ability to use the galleries as teaching stations where demonstration, audio-visual presentations, and interactive computer terminals

Above: Top, Jefferson and Franklin exhibition by Ray and Charles Eames; bottom, figure of an archer from the battle of Towton in the War gallery.
Opposite: Line drawings showing the development of gallery designs, on the left early proposals and on the right later ideas; from the top, the War gallery, the Self-defence gallery, the Oriental gallery and the Tournament gallery.

SELF DEFENCE

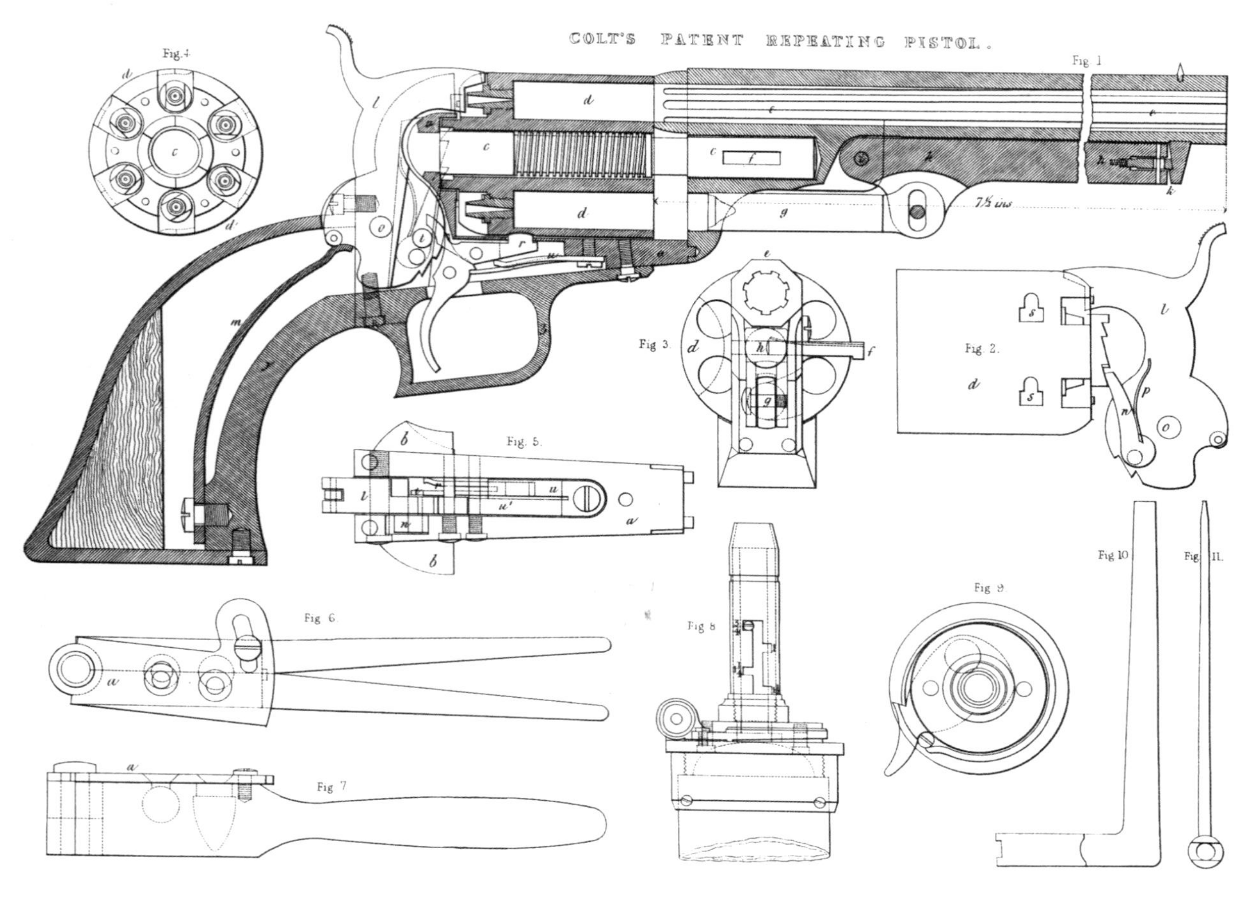
COLT'S PATENT REPEATING PISTOL.
Fig. 1
Fig. 2.
Fig. 3
Fig. 4
Fig. 5.
Fig. 6.
Fig. 7
Fig. 8
Fig. 9
Fig. 10
Fig. 11.

enrich immeasurably the visitors' knowledge and perception of the subject.

This search for enriched interpretation provided the most rewarding aspect of the project for me, combining as it did the dual role of lead designer and latter-day Diaghilev. The former task offered many of my colleagues and myself the unusual opportunity to design at many different scales from the macro-scale of master planning to the micro-scale of showcase and furniture design. The second underwrote, with Guy Wilson, the artistic direction of the project – the recruitment and interaction with a team of consultants, advisers, artists, modelmakers and designers who have all contributed their individual skills to our mutually choreographed concept.

This in essence is what the process of design is all about – the ability to orchestrate a diverse group of individuals and realise a product that is seamless, coherent and thought through in every detail. It is about dialogue, argument and restraint. Ideas are usually overabundant on this kind of high-profile project. The key is to control the tendency to over-elaborate or overwork the constituent parts – inject drama where it is most relevant, vary the pace of presentation to enliven the visit, place seating where it is most appropriate, connect to the outside with strategically placed viewing areas, allow for overlooking and the axial view, provide areas for perambulation; create sanctuaries for quiet study, as well as theatrical settings for demonstration and the animated sets. In reality we have provided a building with an in-built support system for the collection manifest in the Education Department, the Library, the cinemas and the Newsroom. The detailed planning and visual setting of each gallery also further the support system by providing a rich overlay of interactive elements, demonstration areas and audio-visual presentations.

Museums have to become very different animals if they are to succeed in a world continually bombarded with visual imagery. They have to work at many levels, using a multimedia approach, if they are to appeal to the variety of visitors which it is their duty to attract.

The most influential guidelines for the museum's conceptual base were developed in the early dialogue with James Cooke, Guy Wilson and myself for *Strategy 2000*, the document supporting the argument for a new national museum building for the Royal Armouries. These guidelines I think have been implemented in full – however, their success is for the public to decide, but if their opinion mirrors the pleasure and delight the collaboration with the Royal Armouries has had for the design team, we will have succeeded.

Those who have read *The art of memory* by Frances Yates will know that the ability to hold an experience is rooted in our recollection of places and things. There is plenty of evidence that our topographical memory contributes decisively to our capacity of recall – so I leave the last word to Gombrich who recalled in his paper, *The museum, past, present and future:*

> The story of an old gentleman who could walk through the Louvre in his mind as an example of *prodesse*, the lasting profit we gain by remembering a collection. I know full well that the veritable bugbear of the exhibition age is the so called static collection where nothing is allowed to be changed or shifted. I don't want to overstate the case for this arrangement wherever we are sure we can do better. But I should like to remind enterprising curators in the museum world that among the many difficult skills which are demanded of them the one which calls for the most noble sacrifice is the great art of leaving well alone.

Above: Details of mail and plate armour from the Oriental collection.
Opposite: Top and bottom, presentation boards used for the selection of materials for the exterior (top) and interior (bottom) of the museum; centre, British patent drawing of a Colt percussion revolver.
Following pages: Plans and elevations of the museum and painting by Carl Laubin of a section through the museum.

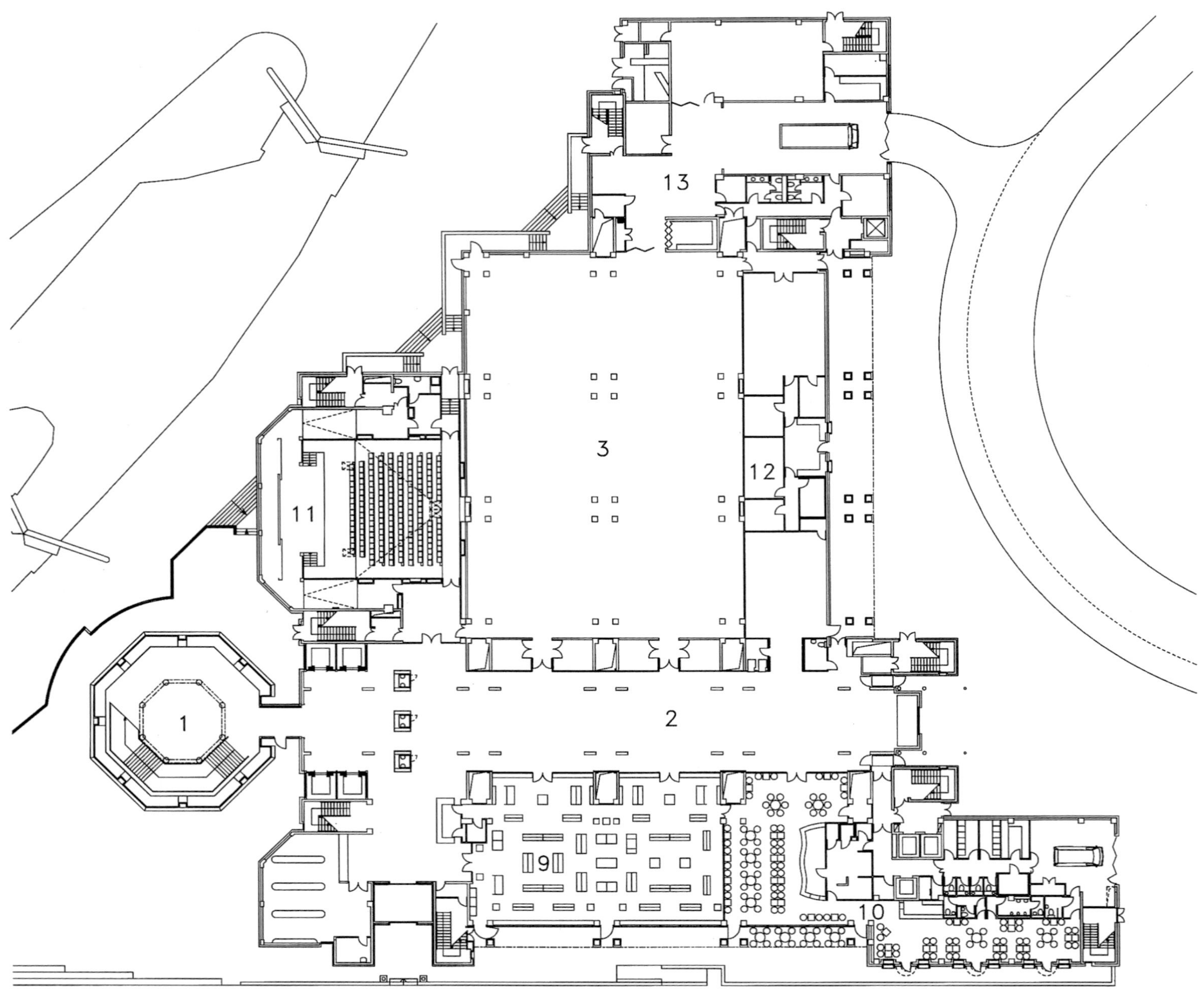

GROUND FLOOR

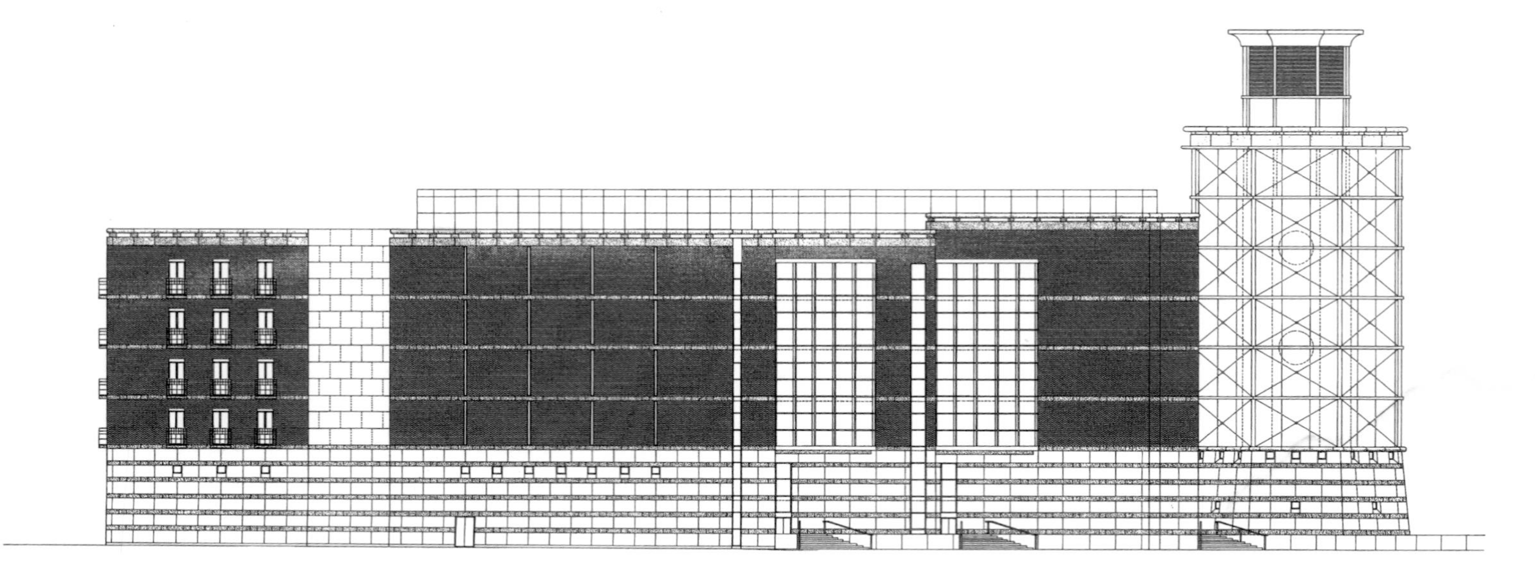

EAST ELEVATION

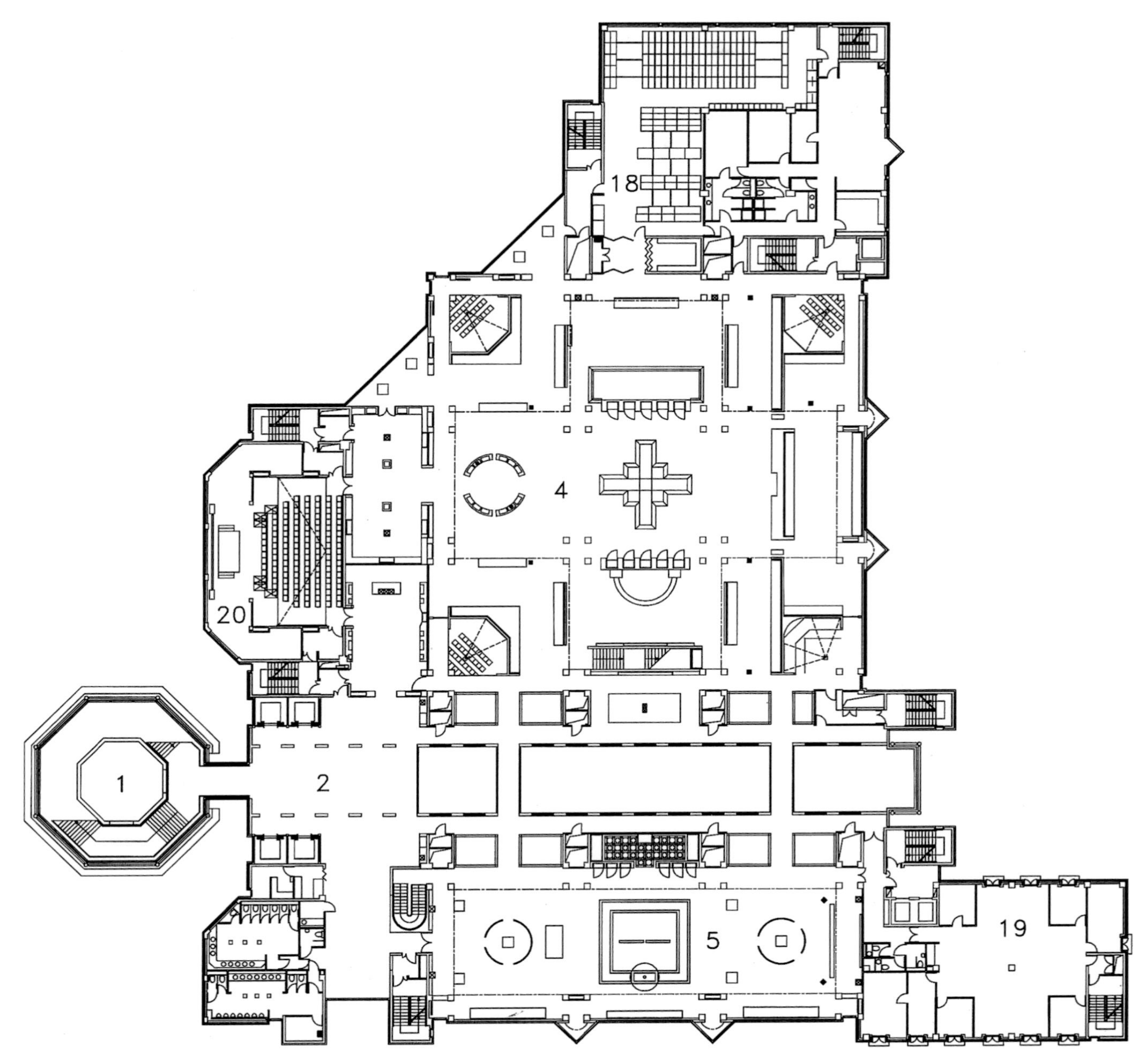

FIRST FLOOR

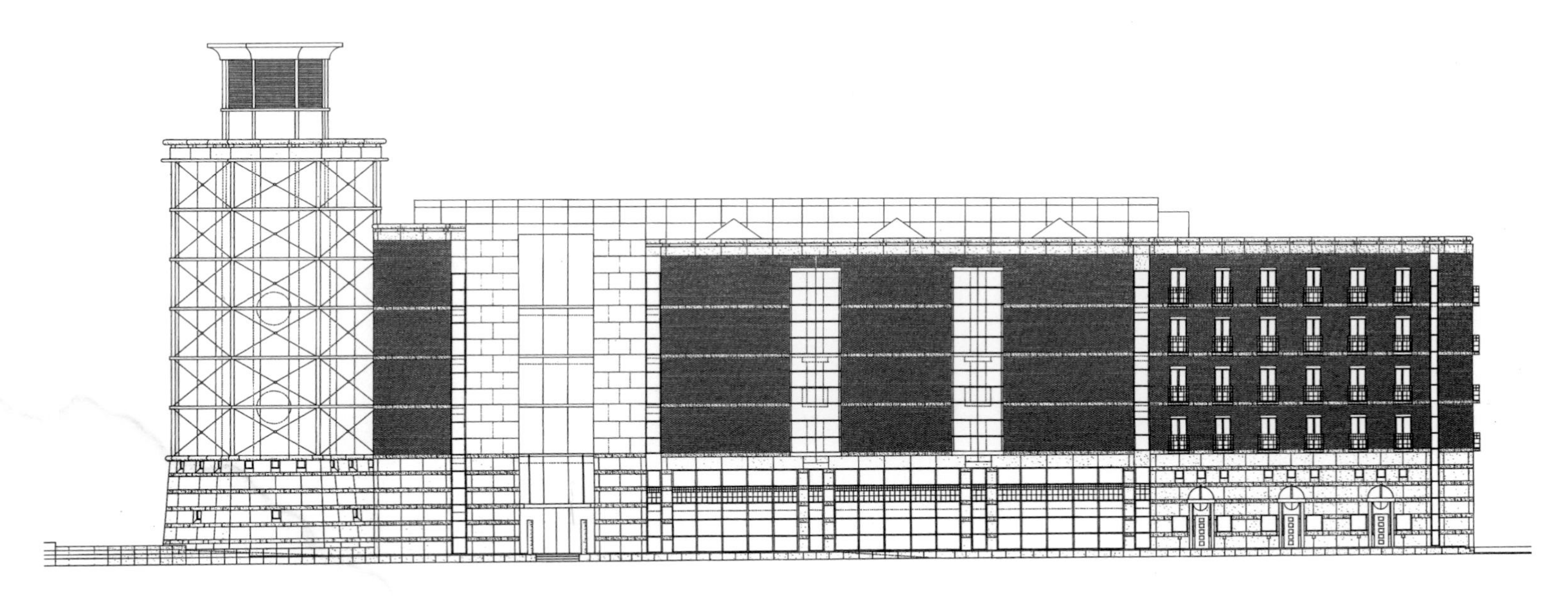

WEST ELEVATION

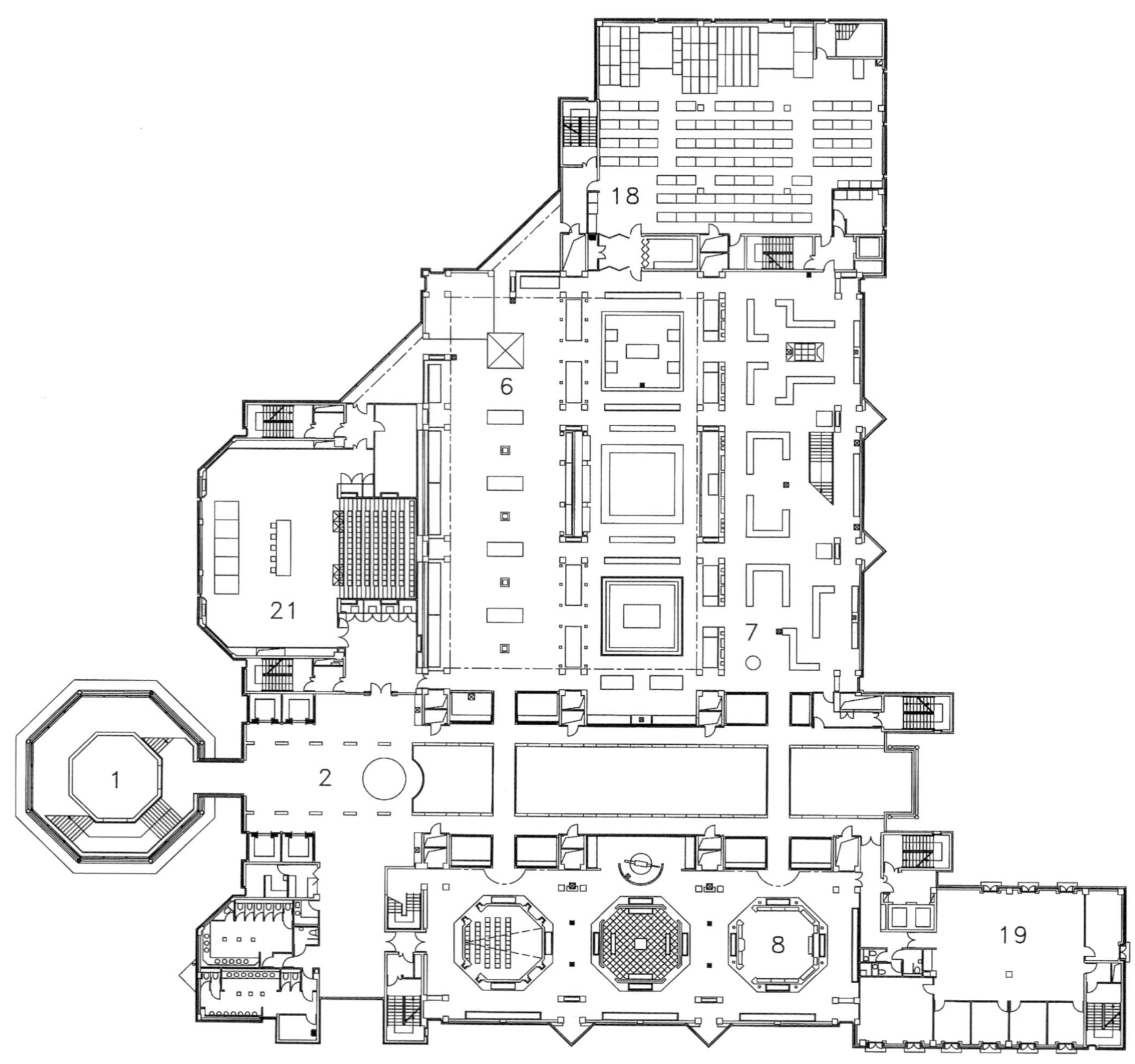

SECOND FLOOR

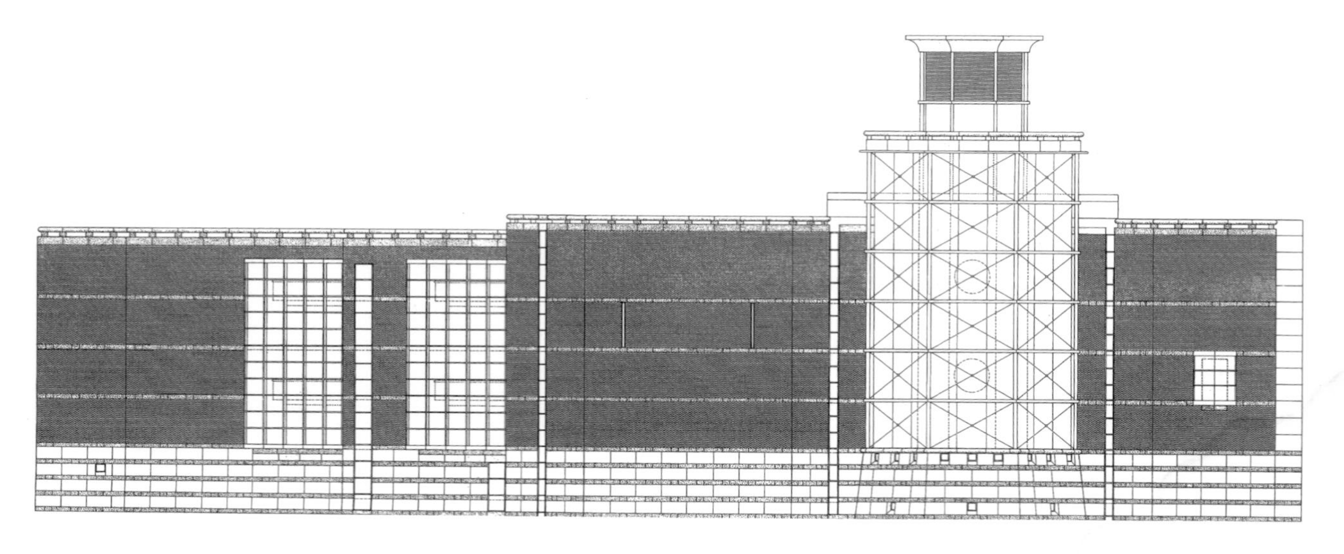

NORTH ELEVATION

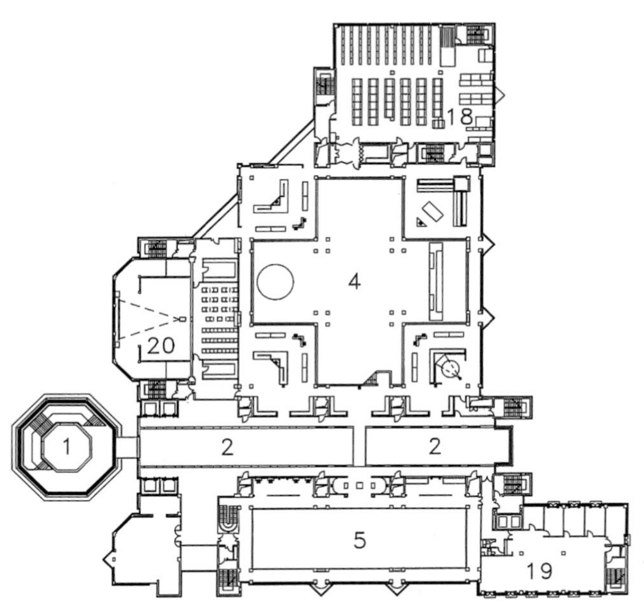

FIRST FLOOR MEZZANINE

SECOND FLOOR MEZZANINE

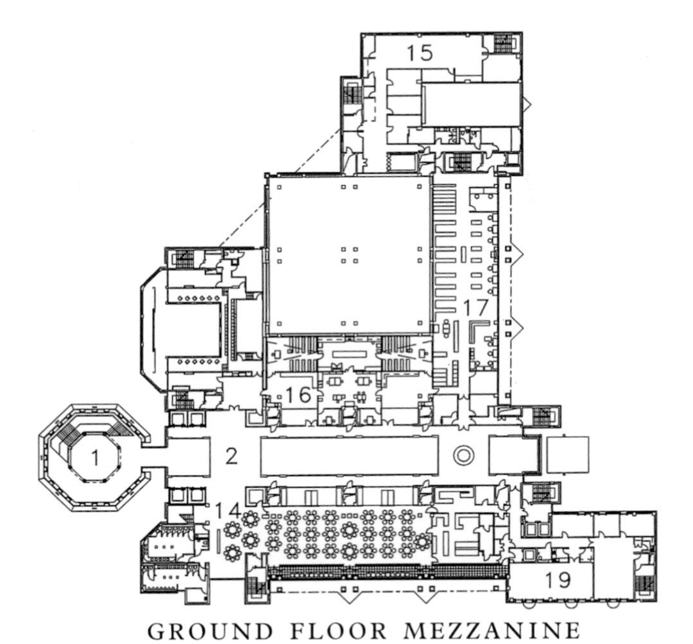

GROUND FLOOR MEZZANINE

1 Hall of Steel
2 The Street
3 Temporary gallery
4 War gallery
5 Tournament gallery
6 Oriental gallery
7 Self-defence gallery
8 Hunting gallery
9 Museum shop
10 Bistro
11 Cinema
12 Photographic studio
13 Exhibition preparation
14 Restaurant
15 Conservation
16 Education
17 Library
18 Storage
19 Offices
20 War cinema
21 Newsroom
22 Plant room

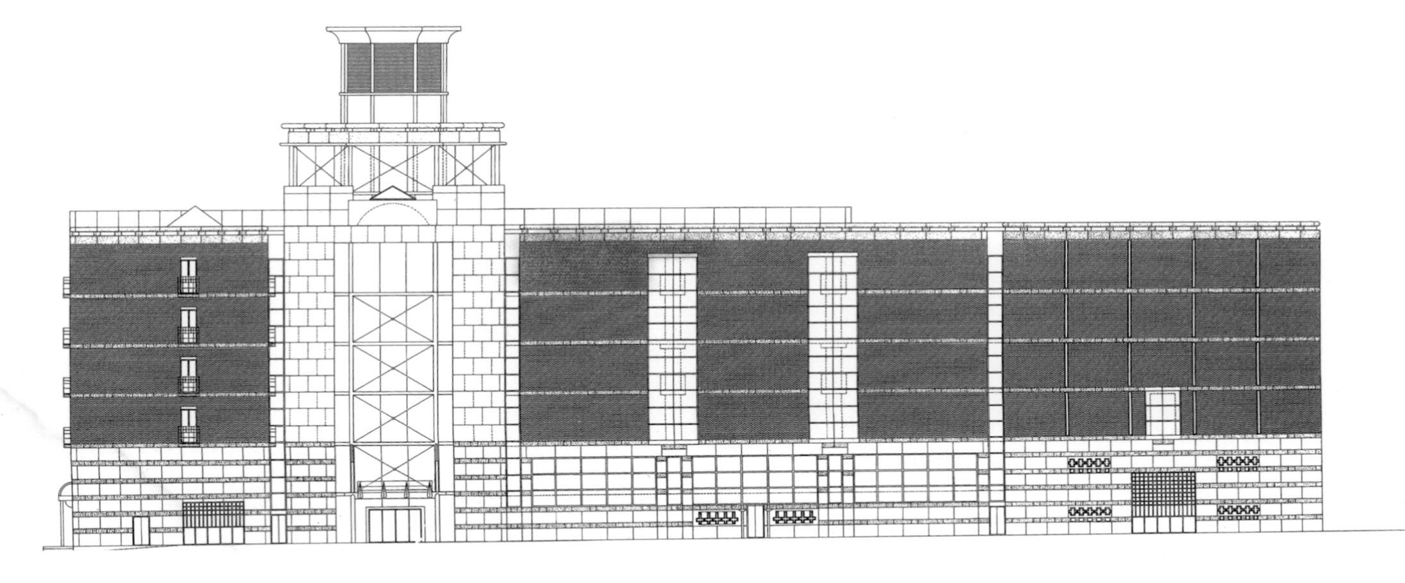

SOUTH ELEVATION

A MUSEUM FOR TH
NO WAR OR BATTLE'S SOUND · WAS HEARD THE WO

WATERLOO
1815

ORIENTAL
TOURNAMENT
OYAL ARMOURIES
THE IDLE SPEAR AND SHIELD WERE HIGH UPHUNG

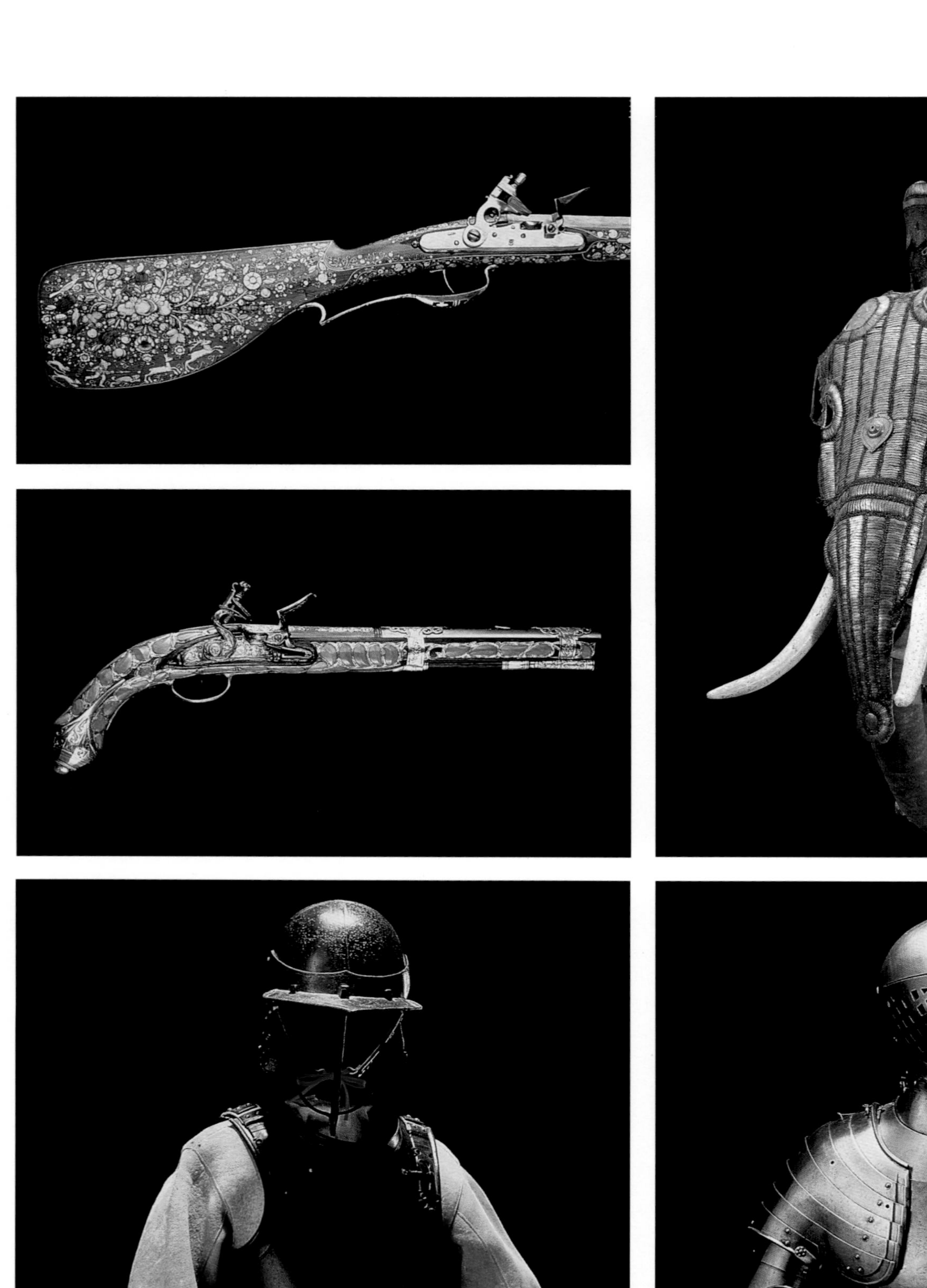

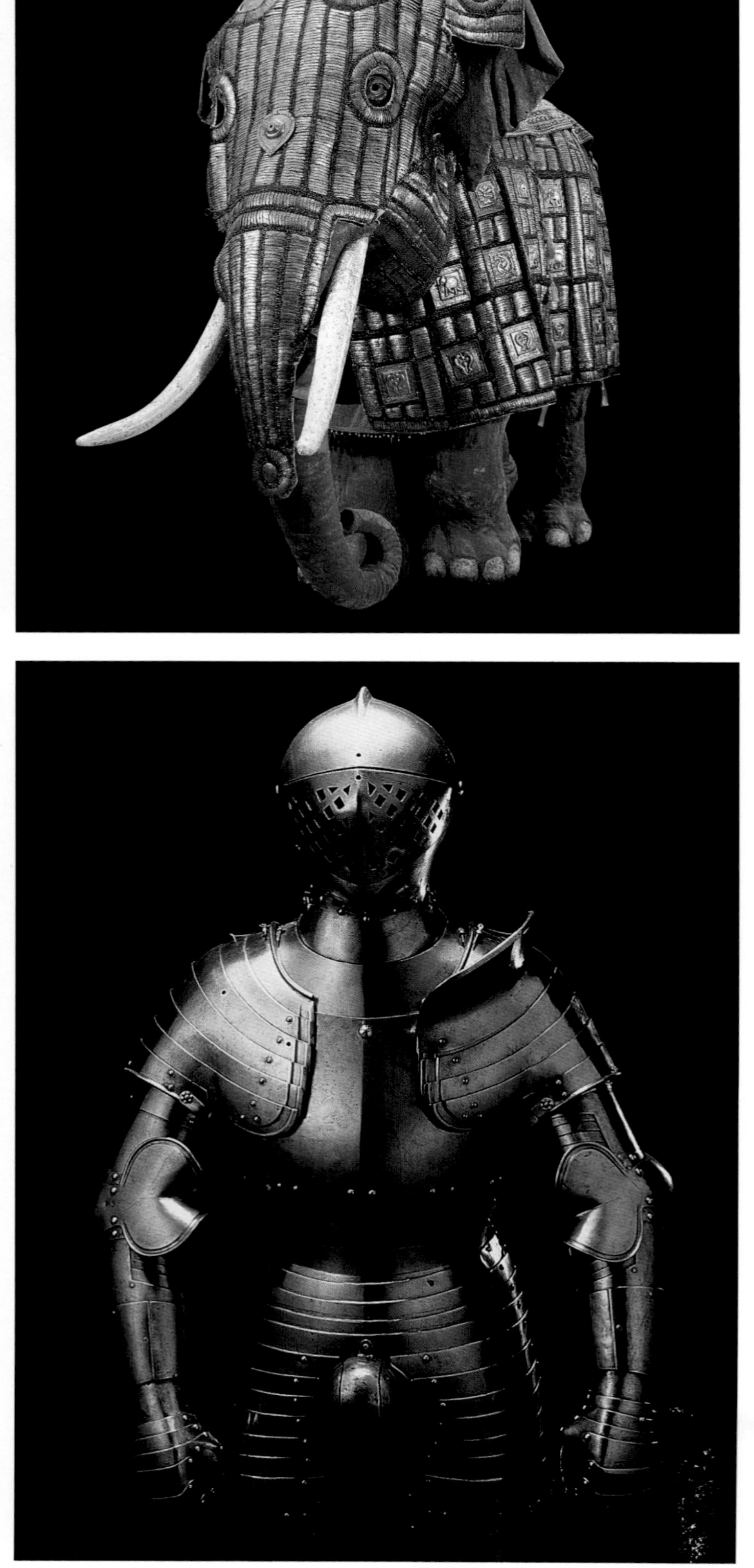

The curators

GUY WILSON

The powerhouses of any museum display or exhibition are the curators, the museum professionals whose love and knowledge of their collections is the essential ingredient on which everyone else in the creative team feeds. How much more true this is for an entirely new museum all those of us involved have now discovered.

In this project the curators were given a difficult task – to create in just over two years five major galleries using a multiplicity of display and interpretative techniques, many of which were new to them, in order to show the museum's collections in a very different way.

Every idea, every decision, every move needed and got curatorial input. Every consultant came to rely upon the knowledge and skills of the curators. As a result the workload was phenomenal. One day displaying objects in traditional fashion, the next selecting illustrations, the next in costume on a film set, the next writing labels, the next researching a detail of the costuming and equipping of one of the many life-like figures, the next agonising over what to leave out of a film script, the next advising on the storage of collections in the new museum, the next working on a computer interactive programme, the next begging or borrowing something we did not have but needed, and sometimes having to juggle with most of those and many others in just one day.

Each of the five galleries has had its own team and its own team leader, or gallery co-ordinator, but because the staff of the Royal Armouries is small most were involved in more than one gallery. The teams met together regularly to discuss progress and sort out problems, and all reported direct to the Master of the Armouries as artistic director. Each gallery team worked to a brief and blue-print which had been developed in conjunction with them by the design team and the Master over months of often late-night discussions in that period before the future of the project was certain.

Thousands of objects to display, over 200 showcases to fill, over 50 films, audio-visual and computer programs to develop, and many figure scenes to advise on and dress. None of us involved had in our careers been exposed to such pressure over such a long period of time. To channel and record the enormous burgeoning of creativity systems had to be developed in areas in which they had never before been necessary. Try keeping track of 5000 labels and 3000 illustrative graphics in your head. It can't be done. So our computerised collections-management system was adapted to record both the packing and movement of collection objects to Leeds and the selection, ordering and receipt of graphic material; and systems for the approval, setting and printing of labels were developed.

The curators, who were appointed for their knowledge of arms and armour, were expected overnight to become more general historians, capable of putting their collections into a social or technical context which would make them more interesting to the visiting public. So the curators responsible for the Hunting gallery had to learn, for instance, about modern techniques for conserving big game in Africa, while their colleagues in the War gallery

Above: Portrait of Alexander Popham, English school, about 1650; Japanese armour presented to James I by Tokugawa Hidetada in 1613.
Opposite: Treasures of the collection: left from top, flintlock sporting gun, Alsace, 1646; flintlock pistol, Algerian, late 18th century; harquebusier armour, English, about 1650; right from top, elephant armour, Indian, about 1600; foot combat armour of Henry VIII, English, about 1520.

were scripting a film on the disasters and successes of the Crimean War, and the curators in the Self-defence gallery were learning about how modern police forces actually use their defensive and offensive equipment. Time did not allow errors to be corrected as they all worked under the tremendous pressure of knowing that they had to get it right first time.

In the process we all were faced with questions to which we did not know the answers. Every curator was stretched by the process and learnt more about the subject and about him- or herself in the process. When faced with displaying an armour for the first time on a naturalistic man and horse, our lack of knowledge of costume and horse furniture was sometimes exposed. When on a film-set recreating a battle or the use of a particular weapon, again there were times when a lack of knowledge was sometimes painfully exposed or a thoughtless assumption laid bare. The museum and the curators will be better in future for the experience. It will help us all to do our jobs better in the years to come and to take advantage of what we have created

And it should be remembered that all this was done by a staff of only ten curators in addition to all their normal work of responding to the needs and requests of the public and at a time when the Royal Armouries' museum of artillery was being completed at Fort Nelson and plans were being drawn up for the redisplay of the Royal Armouries in the Tower. It was done, too, at a time of considerable personal disruption. Most were relocating and had to find a new house and move while the pressure was greatest. For some the opening of the new museum marked the end of their career with us as they decided to stay in London or move on elsewhere. For others they had to prepare for life in the Tower without the rest of us. But whatever their circumstances all the curators gave wholeheartedly of their best with almost unerring good humour throughout the stresses and strains of what will almost certainly be the most intensely creative period of their lives.

Above: Illustrations from one of the graphic walls in the Tournament gallery, *Young knights of the empire* and *Britian needs you at once*.
Left: Design sketch for the early whaling case.
Opposite: Curators, designers and the mounting team working on the showcase layouts and installations.

Approach to education

PETER HAMMOND

Since all museums exist to care for and exhibit their collections and to research and impart knowledge of them, they have always had an educational function, in that they make learning possible for those who are interested. The modern museum also has an educational purpose, actively to promote learning among all who may potentially visit or use it.

When the Royal Armouries began to consider the place of education in its new museum, it was able to draw on more than 20 years experience in which the museum had developed and defined its educational mission. In 1974 it set up an education service at the Tower to provide for the thousands of school groups who were already coming there for serious study. They were coming both to the Tower itself and to the Royal Armouries, and our education service therefore served both the historic site and the museum within it. The common approach was learning first hand from the real thing and stimulating curiosity, imagination and debate as well as imparting information.

At first the focus was on history but with the development of the National Curriculum, the education service took on new subjects such as English, art and design, maths and science and technology. It also helped pioneer the use of drama in museum education, through theatre-in-education. The key principle of active learning at first hand also guided the response to the wide range of needs, skills and interests among the pupils who came to the Tower. Learning could be an enriching experience for everyone, and fun as well.

From the beginning, because of the Tower's popularity, the Royal Armouries' education service could never provide directly for every visiting pupil. For most, the service had to work by helping their teachers with advice, information and learning materials, so that they could best plan their own visits. Regular in-service training courses developed as well as work with teacher-training institutions. Staff also went out to run courses in teacher's centres, schools and colleges.

Just as the education service continued to draw on the expertise of other museum staff, in developing programmes and learning materials, so it increasingly contributed its own special knowledge of how learning takes place in the museum. Education staff advised on display design and on how visitors with disabilities might be given access to the collections.

Meanwhile, the education service quickly extended its scope to adult education and informal leisure learning. Academic experts as well as the museum's own curators and conservators contributed to evening study courses and weekend workshops and the Royal Armouries joined forces with other adult-education providers such as the Historical Association. For less formal leisure learning by younger visitors, there were gallery talks and individual programmes in the Education Centre.

The education service also began to reach our to children in special schools or hospitals who could never expect to visit the Tower and the Royal Armouries, taking out objects for them to enjoy and appreciate.

All these developments reflected not only the growing experience and resources of the Education Centre at the Tower but also a growing awareness

Above: Top, illustrated manuscript showing foot combat with pollaxes, French, about 1475; bottom, making the introductory film for the Tournament gallery.
Opposite: The museum education programme involves interaction, interpretation, demonstration, learning, enjoyment and participation.

throughout the museum world of the potential of museums for education. When planning for Leeds got under way, the time had come to define the Royal Armouries' educational role in the light both of experience and those developing expectations.

The Royal Armouries education policy, entitled *A museum for learning*, sets out the museum's education mission:

> To provide the widest possible range of learning opportunities based upon the unique educational resources provided by its collection and the knowledge of its staff, and to encourage and support the widest possible take-up of these opportunities.

The Royal Armouries commits itself to 'providing learning opportunities for every visitor and for all its potential publics, in the local communities which it serves, as well as nationally and internationally', and 'to continue to improve its understanding of the learning needs of all whom it can serve . . . and to find ways to involve the whole museum in providing the widest possible range of learning experiences'.

The policy emphasises 'the unique opportunities of collection-based learning. The interaction of people and objects makes possible learning which is open to all on their own terms'. At the same time it recognises that the Royal Armouries must work 'to break down all barriers to visiting, understanding and enjoying the museum . . . such as those which may be caused by culture and language, age and gender, and disadvantage and disability', and also 'any misperception or prejudice that may prevent a proper appreciation of the collections'.

As the museum's education staff sat down to plan for the new museum in Leeds, they recognised a unique opportunity, but also two formidable challenges. The first challenge has been to set up within just over two years an education service of the scope and standing that had been developed at the Tower over 20 years. The second has been to create an awareness throughout the region of what the education service had to offer and so from the outset make the new museum a major attraction for educational visits. At the same time, there is the unique opportunity to create an education service for a museum which from the beginning had been conceived as an environment for active learning.

First, there is the Education Department, with accommodation for a wide range of users and activities. There are two large fully equipped classrooms, for use both by the museum's own teachers and by visiting school teachers

with their own classes. Both have access to the handling collection of original and replica objects which is stored in the Education Department. An art studio specialises in three-dimensional constructions, based on the study of the museum's objects and using soft metals and mesh as well as card and paper. Finally, there is an area dedicated to early learning and special needs teaching, which is available for small exhibitions, as a meetings area for community liaison, and as a family learning-centre at weekends.

Second, the Department has easy access to the public areas of the museum, and these have been designed to provide active learning experiences not only for educational groups but for every kind of visitor, through the display of objects in context, the audio-visual and sound sequences, the use of live interpretation and demonstration within the galleries, the Newsroom, and the theatres for film and live performances, as well as events in the Tiltyard and activity in the Craft Court and the Menagerie Court.

Overcoming the challenges and taking up the opportunities which the new museum presented has required immensely hard work, imaginative thinking and careful planning. The outcome has been a new education service which combines long experience with innovative approaches and up-to-date facilities. It offers an exciting and imaginative programme for a broad spectrum of interests and needs, in schools and colleges, adult education, leisure learning among visitors, and in the community. It is already assured that these opportunities are being keenly taken up by all its potential users.

The vision set out in the museum's education policy is now realised in a museum where the desire to learn is stimulated by a unique blend of learning experiences, from watching and listening to touching and doing. With the support of the museum's education staff, these experiences will be developed to take account of the differing needs and interests, age and gender, language, culture and ethnicity among the museum's visitors and within its neighbouring communities.

The Royal Armouries in its new museum in Leeds will be a museum for learning through the 21st century.

Above: Top, the crossbow-shooting gallery; left and opposite, sketches for graphic wall displays of the American Civil War displays in the War gallery.
Opposite: Top, the whaling cannon in the Hunting gallery; bottom, demonstration in the Tournament gallery.
Following pages: Concept boards for all the galleries and the Newsroom; centre, scenes from the *Triumph of Maximilian*.

ELIZABETHAN
WORLD

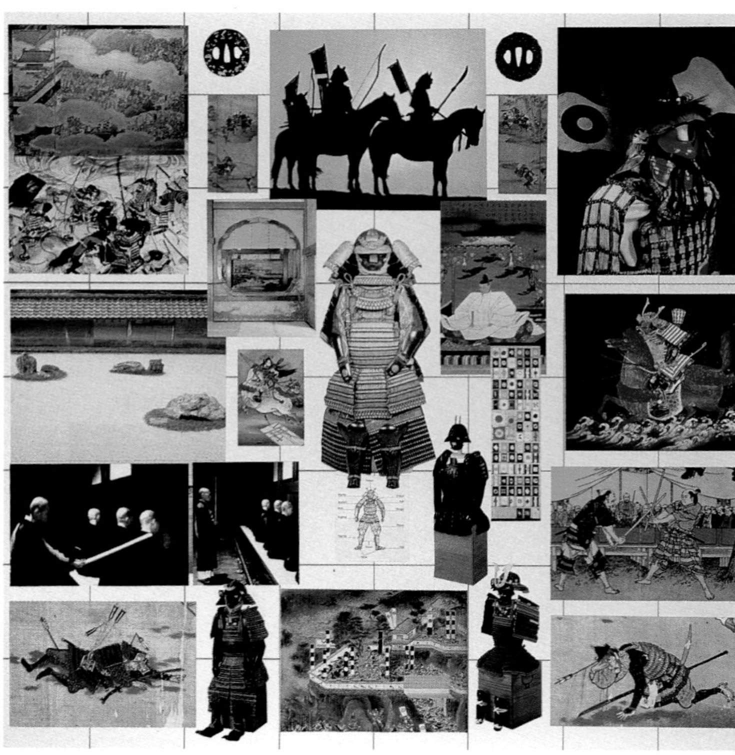

9. The Nuclear Age
TIME
VIET NAM
TEN YEARS LATER
SPECIAL ISSUE
TIME
WAR
IN THE GULF

SPORTSMEN AGAINST HUNGER
EGLINTON
THE SUNDAY TIMES magazine
STAR WARS
Face to face over space
TIME
FLASH POINT
HIC HAROLD MARE NAVIGAVIT
TIME
Northern Ireland
FIRE AND FURY

TOURNAMENT
THE WILD WEST
MYTH & REALITY

WAR

HUNTING
SELF DEFENCE
ORIENTAL
SHOP

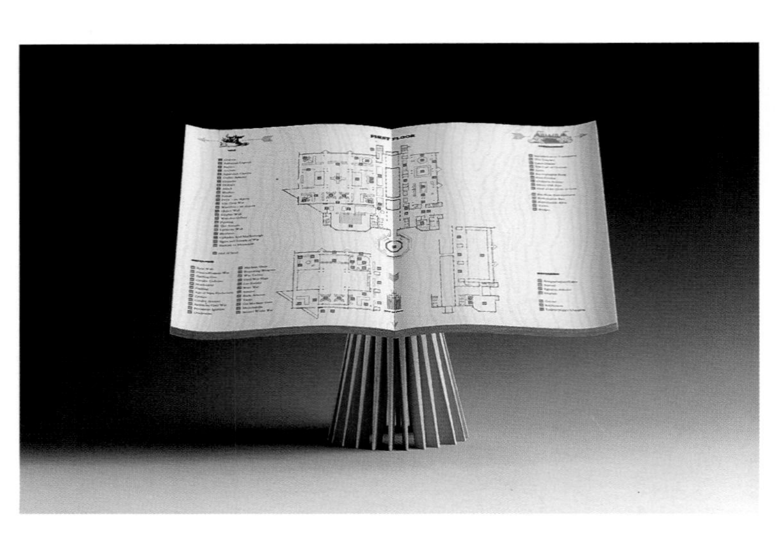

TILT YARD
MENAGERIE COURT
CRAFT COURT

The museum graphics

DEREK WALKER

The selection of Minale Tattersfield to develop the visual identity for the Museum was a great personal satisfaction. My practice had worked from time to time with them since 1971, and Brian Tattersfield and I had also taught together at the Royal College of Art. The complementary nature of their work and the wit and sharpness of their graphic style was very much in keeping with our ambitions for the project. They have the gift of understatement and Tattersfield's absorbing interest in architecture made collaboration both enjoyable and constructive.

The building had been designed to give the visitor an instant appreciation of its general configuration – all the public domain is accessible from the main entry axis – the public Street. It was therefore possible to construct a scenario for signing inside and outside the building that minimised the proliferation of information clutter and developed a formal signing language that used the trappings of tournament and masque for expression. This unique blend of appropriate image and appropriate housing is carried through to the galleries themselves.

The design team developed a unique character for each gallery, placing the objects in context and reinforcing their importance by providing additional information using a wide variety of techniques, film, interactive programmes, transparency walls and graphic walls. We also developed a precise system for the placement of text panels, captions and artwork. This task has been the most intricate and intense challenge for the display team. It has been dependent on reworking the display layouts, layering each set piece with the appropriate settings, visual inserts and text panels which effectively describe the character of each segment of each gallery's presentation.

The real merit of an integrated design team is the osmosis that allows ideas to emerge from constructive debate between the client and the designers. Two specific manifestations of this osmosis are a shooting gallery in the Self-defence area and the *Sight and sounds of war* in the War gallery.

The crossbow-shooting gallery is housed in the setting of a medieval fayre, an amalgam of a castle landscape from illuminated manuscripts and an idyllic woodland world. The targets provided are birds, small animals and eight characters from medieval mythology. This heady mix placed demands on the family Tattersfield, Brian, his wife Mary and daughter Jane, comparable to orchestrating an Inigo Jones masque. It has also stretched the inventive and technical skills of the architects and modelmakers to the limit. The *Sights and sounds of war* is a solemn room dedicated to the human experience of war – the poetry, prose, music and sounds of war. It provided a quite different challenge – combining the physical juxtaposition of the laser-cut steel symbol of the War gallery dramatically lit and placed over a base of endless mirror images of memorial crosses to create a powerful setting for a sound and light show. This elevates museum graphics to another plane . . . a subtler insert of colour and heraldry that hints always at the origins of the imagery but teases the observer as to whence it was derived.

Above: Banners for the Street and Tiltyard designed by Minale Tattersfield.
Opposite: Banners, clock, gallery maps, entry columns, model of the Street and directional arrow and external signing.
Following pages: The family of museum graphics designed by Minale Tattersfield.

WAR

ORIENTAL

SELF DEFENCE

CRAFT COURT

NEWS ROOM

MENAGERIE COURT

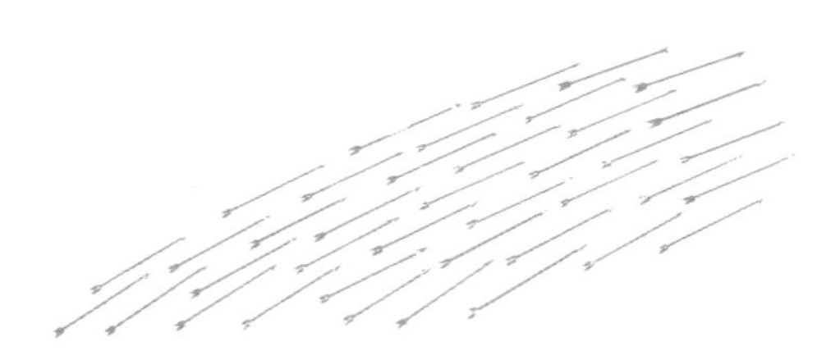

AGINCOURT THEATRE

SIGHTS AND SOUNDS OF WAR

SCHOOL PARTIES

CRECHE

HALL OF STEEL

HUNTING

TOURNAMENT

EDUCATION

DOWN

FRIENDS OF THE MUSEUM

CLOAKROOM

TOILETS

INFORMATION

UP

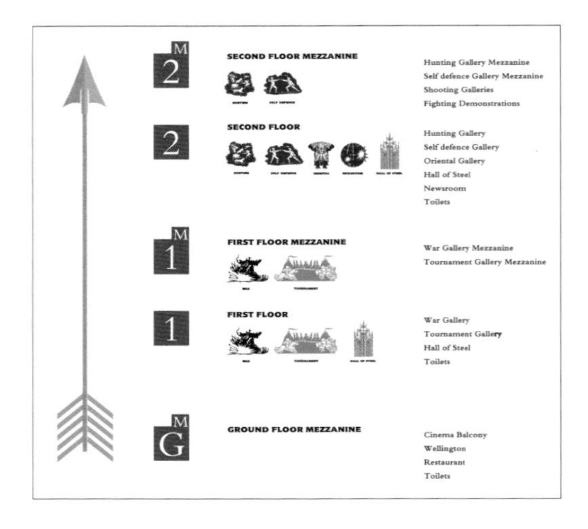

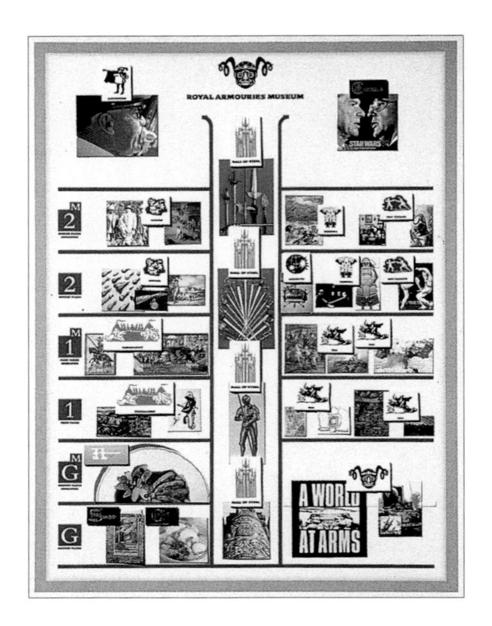

Typography

ABCDEFGHIJKLMNOPQRSTUVWXYZ
ICONE BLACK

ABCDEFGHIJKLMNOPQRSTUVWXYZ
abcdefghijklmnopqrstuvwxyz
Syntax Bold

ABCDEFGHIJKLMNOPQRSTUVWXYZ
abcdefghijklmnopqrstuvwxyz
aBembo

The visual identity

BRIAN TATTERSFIELD

A successful identity is like a good painting, building, piece of music or a perfect meal. It is the manipulation of self-imposed constraints. These stem from deciding on an appropriate 'language' or 'recipe' to express the subject and applying it with disciplined consistency, not necessarily through repetition, but so that each element complements the other.

The subject of arms and armour is one of extreme contrasts. On the one hand is the functional and decorative beauty of the artefacts, linked with the colour and imagery of heraldry and uniforms. On the other is the horror of violence and death.

Finding a common style to convey these opposing qualities was the major problem in creating the identity. The idea of the silhouette was the answer. Two hands casting shadows on a wall can be frightening, while the same hands making the shadow of a rabbit are fun.

Taking this principle with the addition of colour, it was possible to create a sombre and violent symbol for War, while producing a much more light-hearted one for Tournament.

Most of the images are taken from historical references, then transformed into simple graphic silhouettes.

It was particularly difficult to decide on an image which could symbolise the whole museum, but it soon became obvious that one object in the collection embodied all the elements that were to be portrayed in the museum. This was a remaining piece from a suit of armour made by the armourer of German Emperor Maximilian I and presented by him to Henry VIII.The helmet is adorned with curling ram's horns, and has a grotesque mask visor complete with brass spectacles. Beautifully designed and made, it is witty, very threatening and truly sinister. In its simplified form as a symbol it takes on the added quality of timelessness.

There is a symbol for each gallery and all other public areas of the museum. The typeface which accompanies these symbols is a slightly serifed bold letterform Icone Black, while secondary typefaces are Bembo in regular and bold, with Syntax which is used mainly on external signage.

Because of the simplicity of the layout of the building there is little need for a conventional signing system. Instead visitors are directed to the galleries by huge banners which hang the full height of the internal Street. These are made up of sections joined by steel rods with arrows pointing to the levels on which each gallery can be found.

Floor directions are in the form of gigantic open books made of laminated beech and standing on tripods inspired by Renaissance carpentry. Staircases are indicated by fencing figures pointing their swords up or down. Sub-identities have been created in the same style for the bistro and restaurant, using neon lettering derived from illuminated letters where appropriate.

The use of symbols to explain and make clear has been extended into the galleries themselves. In the War gallery, each of the themed areas has its own symbol, such as the the arrow storm for Agincourt and the mushrom cloud for modern war. All is intended to be discreet and yet clear and easy to follow.

Above: Crossbow-shooting gallery images by Brian, Mary and Jane Tattersfield. *Opposite:* The Wellington restaurant, the Nelson bistro, lift signs, decorative pyramids for the Tournament gallery, etched glazed screen and typography.

The theatrical presentations

DEREK WALKER

When Guy Wilson and I discussed the hidden agenda for the museum display, he spoke movingly about his profound wish to communicate his own vivid view of the subject to the public visiting the museum.

Our discussion ranged outside the strait-jacket of conventional museum wisdom, we talked about the power of music and the spoken word, the fusion of the object with a contextual image. We had both experienced the overwhelming effect of a great theatrical production and the influence it can have on the perception of human conflict.

Joan Littlewood's *Oh, What a Lovely War* at Stratford East reflected the essential lunacy of the First World War, with withering condemnation. Peter Hall's *War of the Roses* at the RSC's 400th-anniversary production at Stratford-upon-Avon exposed a theatre audience for the first time to the sound of cold steel and the harsh resonance of a bleak and masterful stage setting. These two seminal productions of the post-war British theatre stayed vividly in our minds as we meticulously sought the team of architects, artists, designers, craftsmen and film-makers we needed to present the objects in a context that was powerful, interactive and consistently informative.

It seemed very natural that I should encourage two old friends and colleagues, John and Elizabeth Bury, to contribute some of their unique skills to the development of certain elements of the display. Ted Happold and I had worked successfully in the past with John Bury on prize-winning theatre designs in two national competitions and, more pertinently, Bury was the magical designer who had created the sets for the *War of the Roses* and *Oh, What a Lovely War.* He is a quite exceptional man of the theatre, one of the handful of designers who lights and costumes all his set designs.

It is important to understand why we wanted to involve a couple whose work had graced stages from Tokyo to London, from New York to Los Angeles from Berlin to Glyndebourne. The reasons were threefold – first, John Bury's roots in Joan Littlewood's popularist theatre workshop which provided his initiation into the theatre. Second, the extraordinary partnership with Peter Hall at the RSC, Glyndebourne, the National Theatre and in the international arena, which moved theatre design into a new era as cerebral and dynamic as Hall's interpretations. And finally Elizabeth Bury's remarkable talents, not only as John Bury's main collaborator since their RSC days, but in her own right as painter, colourist, costume designer and modelmaker.

John and Elizabeth first worked together on Peter Hall's production of Schoenberg's opera *Moses and Aaron,* the first operatic production to hit the *Evening Standard* billboards. '*Orgy Opera Opens*' blazed out on every street corner – camels, elephants, chickens, goats and a frozen bevy of sacrificial virgins snatched the headlines but the working relationship between the Burys blossomed and has flourished ever since.

After the RSC a brief dalliance with Hall at the Royal Opera House and a memorable *Tristram and Isolde* and then to the National Theatre where for nine years Bury was Head of Design. A classic *Volpone* solved effectively for

Above: Elizabeth Bury's study for the tiger-hunt tableau.
Opposite: John Bury's 1964 design for Peter Hall's production of *The War of the Roses.*

BANK
SALOON

the first time the formidable problems of designing on the Olivier stage. *Tamberlaine, The Cherry Orchard, Amadeus*, Schofield's *Othello* and *Strife* were equally successful as were the parallel collaborations with Hall at Glynebourne where *La Callisto, Don Giovanni, Fidelio* and the magical and lyrical *Midsummer Night's Dream* continued the rapport of the two theatrical heavyweights.

The great tragedy of the theatre from a designer's viewpoint is the ephemeral nature of the set, very often little or no documentation, just a vision in the collective memory that is about movement, lighting and atmosphere but not a permanent memorial.

This meant that the Royal Armouries did offer a modest challenge to give a certain permanence to the sets which were developed either to illustrate some pivotal points in the development of technology or to create an atmosphere for an area where demonstration was part of the educational programme of the museum. The painterly backdrops for the *dojo* area, illustrating the Wild West, Downtown Verona, a woodland glade for a duel at dawn, a Japanese gymnasium and a German sabre school were standard fare for Elizabeth Bury.

However, much of their work has been concentrated on more complex gallery installations. The set for the battle of Pavia involved the architects and three of the artists and craftsmen: David Hayes, Gerry Embleton and Bill Gordon. A classical proscenium frames the battle scene of Pavia which took place in mist on frozen swampy ground; it was also one of the first battles in which firearms proved to be the decisive factor.

The *Sights and sounds of war* is a small theatre devoted to images, music, poetry, contemporary descriptions and letters from many fields and periods of human conflict. Elizabeth Bury's moving imagery established a template for the design team's developed construction that provides the setting for the performance. In the final version a sea of crosses, disappearing into infinity, is illuminated beneath the screens during the musical or poetic interludes in the segments of a 90-minute explanation of the various human reactions to war in all its facets.

In the public space adjacent to the Hunting gallery, Elizabeth Bury developed a circular composition for an Indian tiger hunt recreated from a Victorian description. David Hayes produced the animals for the set and Gerry Embleton and Keith Bartlett the figures.

Inside the Hunting gallery the three internal octagons designed by the architects are overlooked from the mezzanine; on them the Burys have developed two sets of very different character. One is a puntgunning scene set in the Essex marshes, a watery inlet with a reflective tranquil surface with foliage above and below the water. On the other the chamois hunt utilised a false perspective of an Alpine rocky outcrop with powder snow and ground frost. Each scene has been beautifully handled. As theatre designers they have an appreciation of the choreography of space; they use lighting in a totally different way from an architect and study the combination of light, colour and texture within a setting to engage dramatically the observer's perception. These very specific skills have been invaluable during the process of design development where instinct is also crucially assisted by experience and precedent. Indeed the contribution of the Burys to the design team has been more significant than the installations. They have also been influential in defining the spirit and animation of the spaces set aside for demonstrations and interaction throughout the museum.

Above: Top, Elizabeth Bury's sketch for the *Sights and sounds of war;* bottom, study for the punt-gunning set.
Opposite: The backdrops for the *dojo* demonstration area by Elizabeth Bury. Top left, *Duel at dawn;* top right, *Japanese garden;* centre, *German sabre school;* bottom left, *Downtown Verona;* bottom right, *The Wild West.*

The art of demonstration

GUY WILSON

Specially trained 'interpreters' have been recruited and trained to work with the collections and subjects of the museum and explain them to the visiting public. These interpreters come from a wide range of backgrounds. Most are actors, all have a love of history, and most could already fight and ride before they came to us. But stage-fighting and 'theme-park jousting' are very different from the reality which we attempt to portray. So whatever their background and however developed their skills our interpreters all have an intensive period of training. Training, scripting and development is a group activity requiring a team capable of working together as a creative unit. The task of creating this team has fallen chiefly to our Director of Live Interpretation, John Waller. John had spent 30 years choreographing fights for stage, film and television, and teaching stage-fighting in the major London drama schools. Without first his encouragement during the development stage of the project and then his professional skills during its establishment the new Royal Armouries would not have been nearly so activity- and demonstration-based as it now is.

There is much that can be done with live interpretation, but there are also many pitfalls. Because the job of interpretation is to help visitors to understand and learn, we rejected the use of first-person interpretation because it seems to alienate rather than attract large numbers of people. Many find it annoying or embarassing when a costumed performer refuses to come out of role or period and 'pretends' to come from another time. We did not believe that this could possibly work in a newly built museum dealing with the full span of history. Therefore in the Royal Armouries the knights in armour or the soldiers in uniform talk to the visitors as themselves not as their characters. They assume a historical persona only for scripted performances.

There is a wide variety of types of interpretation which we are attempting in the museum, each with a special role to play.

First, there is the physical demonstration of how weapons and armours were used throughout the centuries. Outside in the Tiltyard we put on demonstrations of military and sporting skill-at-arms, including jousting, show the development of arms and armour through historical pageants, and show how animals – horses, dogs, and hawks – have worked with man on the battlefield and in the hunting field. Inside there are two areas for major physical demonstrations. First, the foot-combat ring in the Tournament gallery where armoured knights can be seen engaged in the popular sport of foot combat using either sword or pollaxe. Second, the *dojo*, between the Oriental and Self-defence galleries, where a variety of demonstrations ranging from Japanese martial arts to European fencing and duelling are regularly organised. But none of these is overacted for a quick thrill. As far as is possible we show and explain what really happened, sometimes indeed contrasting popular myth with a less dramatic or bloodier reality.

Another major use of interpretation is to make visitors aware of what objects in the collection could do, and what the consequences of their

Above: Top, John Waller, director of the demonstration team (standing); bottom, a fight demonstration in the *dojo* area.
Opposite: One of the museum's interpreters jousting in full plate armour.

production and use have been for nations and individuals. This means characters from the past talking about events which are important to understanding the collections. These vary from an Agincourt soldier and one of Marlborough's infantrymen on his famous march to the Danube reminiscing about being soldiers, to a husband and wife writing letters to each other in the First World War.

The third key function of the interpreters in the museum is explanation. They explain how the objects work and how they were used, either in special handling sessions or after the completion of a demonstration or interpretation when the weapons used are available for the audience to look at and ask questions about. In the War gallery they also explain how battles have been fought by running simple wargames in a specially constructed wargaming area.

Finally the interpreters are responsible for the story-telling and puppetry which introduces the subjects of the museum to the younger visitors.

One area of explanation the interpreters only touch on in passing is how the objects were made, for this the visitor can find out for themselves. Next to the main building is the Craft Court where the visitor can see a selection of craftspeople working at their trades in traditional workshops. These are an armourer working with a traditional charcoal forge, making armours as they were made in the Middle Ages, a gunmaker, making and repairing modern and antique guns, and combining the metal and woodworking trades which have traditionally formed the art of the gunmaker, and a leather-worker, making boots, saddles, and the buff coats that were used by so many soldiers for defence during the Civil Wars of the mid 17th century.

The work of the interpreters is enhanced by the specially acquired and trained animals with which they often work. Between the Tiltyard and the Craft Court is the Menagerie Court where the birds, dogs and horses live. Here visitors can see them at close hand and meet and talk to their keepers and trainers.

The horses are our own, specially selected to represent as accurately as we can medieval war horses. Four of our horses – Fleur, Berwick, Messenger and Gauntlet – are Lithuanian draft horses, specially imported for us. They were chosen because they are of the size and shape to fit our real horse armours, so the sculpted horses within the museum which now carry the armours have been modelled on the real ones we use outside. They are not the massive cart-horses of popular imagination but strong, thick-set horses of just over 15 hands with short, flat backs and strong necks. They have all been carefully trained to ensure that they are comfortable with swords and spears clashing next to their eyes and with the loud reports of firearms shot from just behind their heads.

The hawks, falcons and dogs are provided and worked for us by the Lakeland Bird of Prey Centre, Lowther Castle, near Penrith. They represent the basic types used in hunting: the birds, hawks for taking ground game and falcons for taking game birds on the wing; the dogs, pointers and retrievers used in shooting, and running and scenting hounds used to chase game and bring it to bay. Eventually the museum hopes to institute its own breeding programmes to breed back to the equivalent of medieval types of dog and horse.

In the summer there are demonstrations in the Tiltyard each day. In the winter this is not possible, but the animals still need to be trained and worked and a lucky visitor who braves the weather can catch something of interest.

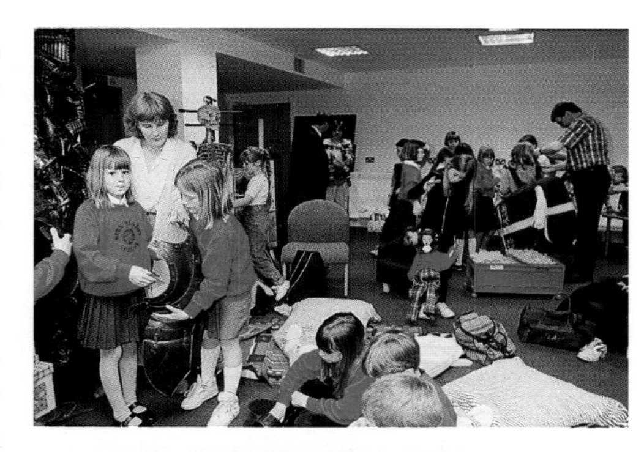

Above: Top, children participating in a handling session in the Education Department; an interpreter demonstrating the use of a Civil War matchlock.
Opposite: Forms of live interpretation used in the museum: top, talking to the public after a demonstration and classroom teaching with objects; bottom, physical demonstrations and story-telling by costumed staff.

HUNTING
RIENTAL

The construction process

DEREK WALKER

When Alfred McAlpine were successful in their bid for the new museum, they had a fair idea of what they were undertaking. They prepared a totally compliant tender, which in terms of design-build terminology meant they had sufficient information, room data-sheets, developed detailed architectural designs, specified materials for the exterior and interior of the museum together with a comprehensive engineering package for the building. Their budget was just within the figure projected by Rex Proctor and Partners, but the complex legal arrangements and cross warranties required between the public and private sector companies, the investors, the Leeds Development Corporation, the Planning Authority and British Waterways, the owners of the site, meant that a considerable slice of the budget had to be reallocated. This was not a popular move for client, contractor or consultants, but what started as an exceptional value-for-money contract had to become 'the minor miracle of Clarence Dock' – minimum depreciation in aspiration, but procured at £2 m less. Herbert Hoover's thesis that 'a good engineer is one who can do for one buck what any fool can do for two' was transferred almost overnight to the contractor.

The design team had been impressed from the start that McAlpine's men on site were precisely those who had appeared at the original contractor interviews. A young team, their enthusiasm and dedication to the project has been manifest since moving on to site in January 1994: Martin Whiteley, Paul Durston, Alan Gardner, Steven Williams, Steve Darlington, Alistair Bewley and Brian Benson have been with the project from the start and they have been involved, as have their consultants Leach Rhodes & Walker, Deakin Callard and Haden Young in translating the detailed designs of Derek Walker Associates and Buro Happold into reality. This has not happened without often violent confrontation on the way, sometimes on a matter of detail, sometimes on alternative choice of material, sometimes selection of a subcontractor or an interpretation of workmanship. It is difficult to adjudicate, as Heery's, RAI's project managers, have found, when deeply held contrary views on matters of procedure, interpretation or sequential release become involved.

This type of contract is certainly historically not the most acceptable for a major national building; surprisingly enough in this case it has worked well by harnessing the single-minded aspirations of all parties enabling them to walk away from the finished product with pride and integrity intact.

This situation owes much to the McAlpine group on site and their backing by senior management. It is an important building and throughout the contract this notion has been reflected by the efforts of McAlpines and their subcontractors.

As is usual, work on this type of old industrial site, is fraught with difficulties. Development has taken place since 1840 when Clarence Dock was constructed. By the early 1900s the site was occupied by timber yards, sawmills and petrol stores.

The presence of ground gases (methane and carbon monoxide) was

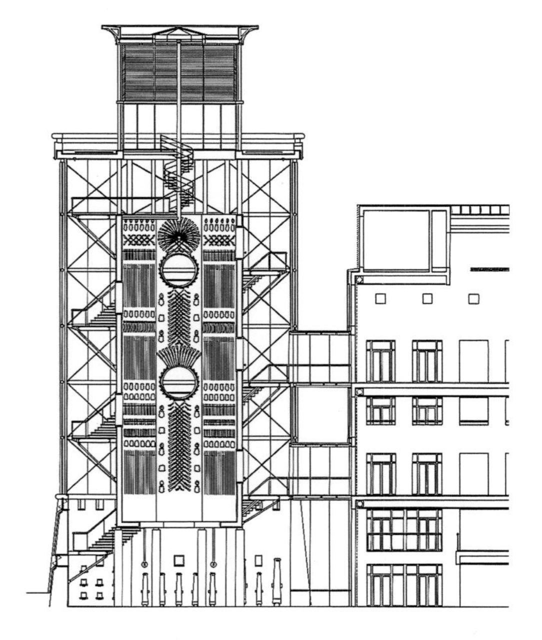

Above: Top, sectional drawing of the Hall of Steel; bottom, a concept sketch of the Street.
Opposite: The Street.

suspected and, following confirmation by ground probing during excavation works, a decision was taken to incorporate a gas-tight membrane into the foundation works at a common level across the site. Below this membrane large pile-caps linking up twenty piles at a time were cast and backfilled using a layer of large single-sized stone through which the gases could permeate. Perforated pipes running through this layer ventilate the gases to the perimeter of the building and into the atmosphere. All areas were blinded with concrete on which the membrane was laid with all joints sealed around all penetrations. Smaller pile-cap foundations and then the main building ground floor slab were cast above the membrane which was also impervious to moisture forming a damp-proof membrane to the ground slab and beams.

The main museum structure was constructed almost as six different buildings: the galleries, the workshop block, the cinema block, the street and ancillary public facilities, the offices and the Hall of Steel. These buildings shared common foundations but once above the ground floor slab depended on each other only for local and lateral support. This strategy allowed construction to progress in different areas at any one time and by July 1994 the offices and workshop block began to form above ground with columns and concrete walls being cast.

The environmental and loading requirements of the collection suggested a massive concrete building. 13600 cubic metres of structural concrete were poured and 1600 tonnes of steel reinforcement incorporated into the main structure. Speed and efficiency of construction was achieved by the use of precast sections for stair flights and floors. Particularly tricky was the casting of the gallery floors and coffered ceilings, which were to remain as exposed concrete. These coffers were formed by casting a concrete plank five coffers long by one coffer wide on a steel mould using a special concrete mix.

The structure of the galleries is integrated closely with the exhibition layout and the level of accuracy demanded has been helped considerably by the precasting element. The planks were cast only 75 mm thick with light reinforcement placed in bays five planks wide, temporarily supported and then integrated as a continuous structure by casting a full concrete slab on top to provide a structural floor. Nine stair towers and three major lift shafts were cast with 200 mm reinforced concrete providing sheer walls and lateral stability to many parts of the building.

The cinema block and Hall of Steel provided the contractors with their most testing challenge. The former had a fixed external plan configuration but varied in layout at each of the three main floors levels and the balcony and projection room of the ground floor cinema were suspended from the structure above. This section had to be cast first then fully supported until the upper structure had been cast and the load transferred.

It took nine months of design effort to solve some unique construction problems posed by the Hall of Steel. The contractors, the architectural and engineering consultants, a specialist steel subcontractor and the world's leading glass manufacturer were stretched to the limit to supply an elegant solution interfacing the steel structure with the glazing.

The structure is very unusual and probably the only one in the world where a double-glazed planar system has been installed internally to a tubular stainless-steel frame. This element of the building with its free-standing concrete inner octagon and glazed linked bridges provided the severest test for the contractors ingenuity and co-ordination skills.

Plastering commenced as the concreting and blockwork elements were

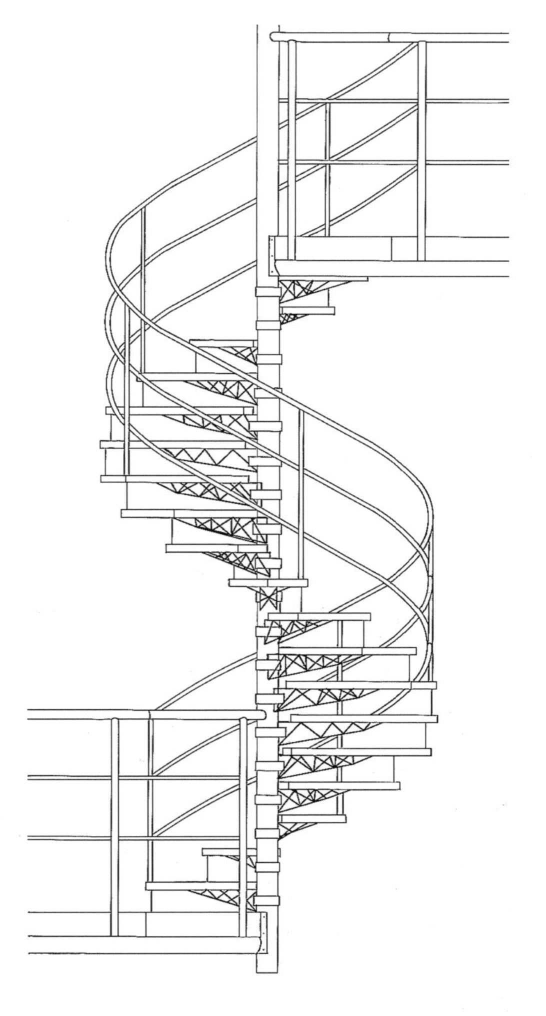

Above: Top, spiral staircase in the lantern of the Hall of Steel; bottom, detail of the Hall of Steel.
Opposite: Work in progress on the site.

completed. Universal projection plaster was proposed for speed of application to the 25,000 square metres of plastering required throughout the museum. The timber flooring for the main galleries also involved extensive procurement and technical research. The architects wanted a good-quality European beech capable of taking the load of many of the displays as well as of accommodating a large number of underfloor electrical services and trunking runs. This installation commenced in July 1995 followed by the installation of shopfitting, showcases and the audio-visual hardware.

The external cladding followed the erection sequence of the frame and wall panels, starting in late September 1994. Three elements were specified for the masonry wall treatments, two storeys of torched blue pearl granite, a metallic dark-blue engineering brick from Baggeridge and a specially developed pre-cast element developed with Tarmac for string courses and parapets. Style Life fixed a specially designed Schuco window system for the great oriels and the riverside glazing and the frames were specified as powder-coated aluminium, coloured light grey to complement the brickwork.

The smaller buildings – the Craft Court, Menagerie and the enclosures of the Tiltyard – used the same palette of materials as the main museum buildings. Similarly the site works use identical colourways for concrete block paving, edgings and brick paviors. A great deal of remedial work also needed to be carried out on the water-edge structures to enable British Waterways to service the renovated dock and the riverside walk.

McAlpine were responsible for the fit-out of the offices, Library, Education Department, storage areas, bistro, restaurant and shop. However their co-ordination role reached a crescendo when the gallery and Hall of Steel fit-outs were undertaken. They were required to programme the work of over 30 subcontractors, plus the Royal Armouries mounting crews, a logistical nightmare that truly become McAlpine's contracting *tour de force.*

The truly remarkable feat is that a complex building type with an equally complex display requirement has been accomplished in a two-year period with weather conditions that were far from perfect towards the end of the contract. It is also significant that the techniques of construction in the museum are not those renowned for allowing a building to be speedily erected. It is difficult to increase the speed of casting concrete, especially when the process of quality monitoring is a principal concern. SCC did well to meet the demanding programme, as did Andrews, the Leeds-based marble and granite company who carried out the external granite cladding and the granite, limestone and decorative slate and marble floors within the building. Each subcontractor has been on a knife-edge during these difficult times for the building industry. We have had to endure our share of bankruptcies and cash-flow problems as legitimate companies with strong building records have gone into decline. The main contractor role is no longer an easy one.

New national museums are very rare birds. Their implementation provides an obstacle course of formidable complexity, security, climatic control, minimum dimensional tolerances, and multifunctional activity. High-quality finishes and an impossible programme made the contractor's role part superman, part psychiatrist. What is certain I am sure is that McAlpines will be delighted to return to less rarified building types – just to get their breath.

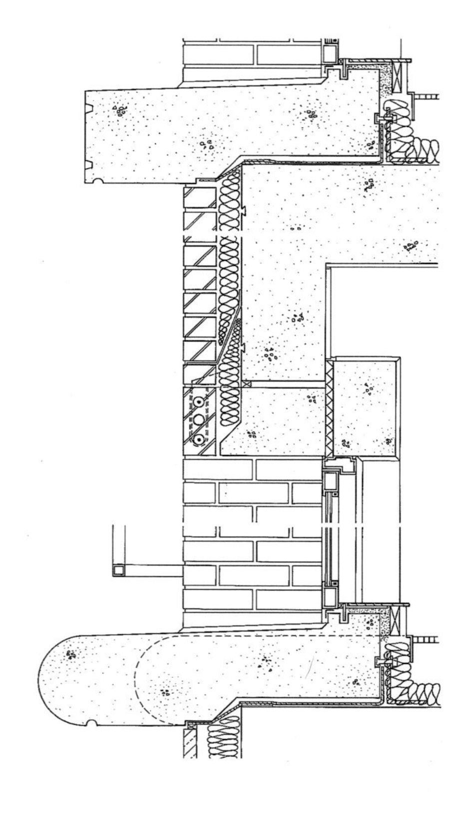

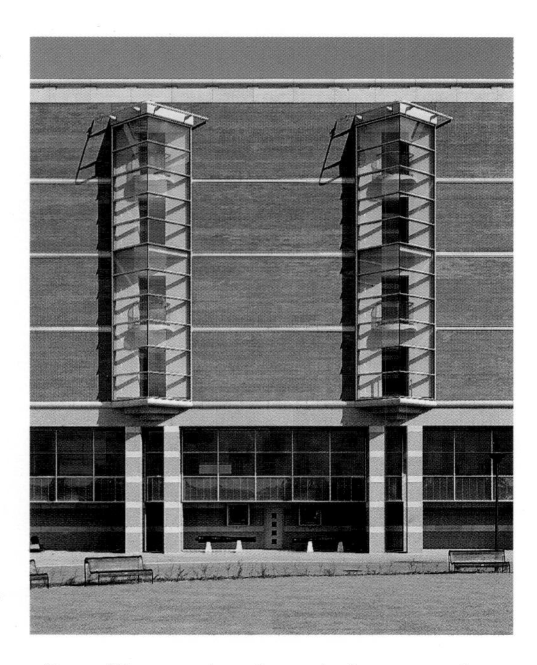

Above: Top, section through the external wall of the office block; bottom, the south facade.
Opposite: Progress shots of the building under construction. Top left, viewed from Clarence Dock; top right, oriel window detail; bottom left, fixing the granite; bottom right, brickwork detail.
Following pages: The lighting-up ceremony of the Yorkshire Electricity Hall of Steel on 11 January 1996.

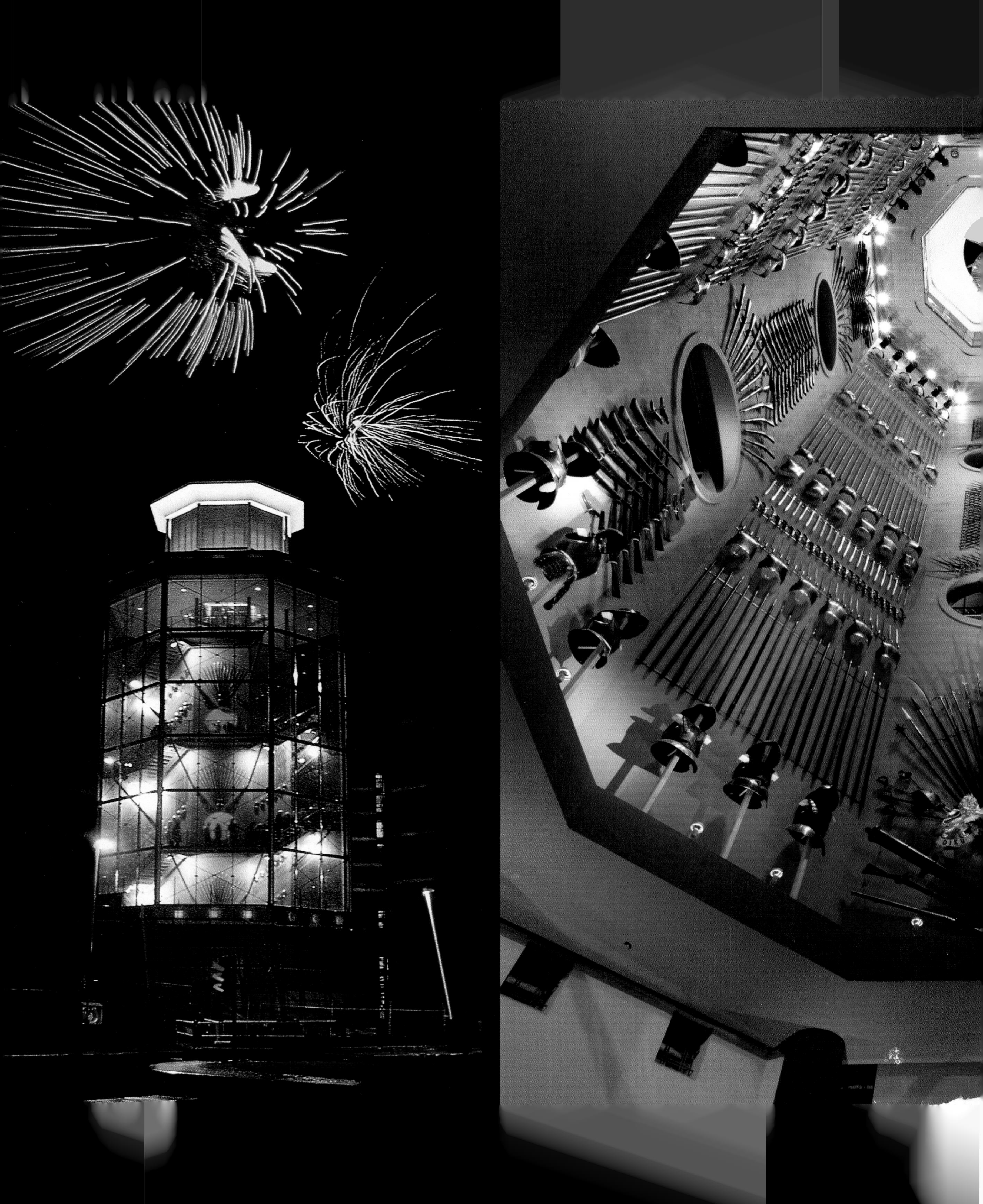

Haden

Structure and servicing

SIR EDMUND HAPPOLD AND ROD MACDONALD

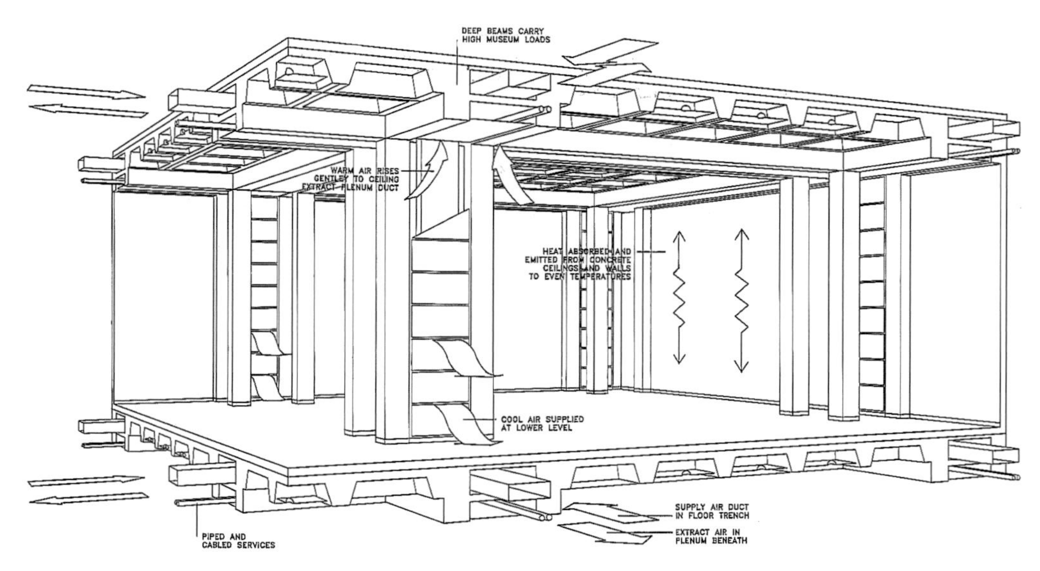

Not surprisingly the profession of military engineering came first with the construction of castles and fortifications. Nowadays, as the Gulf War and Bosnia show, it is more devoted to machinery. But civil and building engineering did not take long to follow with the development of the great cathedrals of medieval times.

Of course cathedral-building was more than engineering. It was an art-form raising emotion through soaring space and the enclosure of light in the service of the development of religious symbolism. This was architecture.

Architectural possibilities however are rooted in engineering invention. Engineering is about organising the design, manufacture, construction, operation and maintenance of any artefact which transforms the physical world around us to meet a recognised need. A service to architecture, effective because it is about economy.

The engineer surveys the site, to discover what is the soil beneath, its exposure, its environment. Here the site is on the side of the old ford across the River Aire, subsequently where the Leeds Liverpool Canal and the Aire and Calder Navigation ended at Clarence Dock. The site is subject to flooding and where once water would have been used to keep people out, now a fortification is needed to keep the water out. A defence wall has been erected right round the museum building on the river side and downstream the ground level of the Tiltyard is raised to 300 mm above the 1949 flood level.

The soil investigation was carried out by drilling boreholes into the ground which showed rubble and waste at the top, then some four to seven metres of river silt and then coal seams and mudstone. Since there had been 100 years of industry there was a risk of contaminated ground though that turned out not to be serious. Some gas was in the ground so the main building was founded on piles into the ground and gas protection measures allowed for.

While the outside of the building has to be defended against the river the inside contains a great number of very valuable exhibits susceptible to deterioration. This calls for a very stable internal level of temperature, air movement and humidity. Light is necessary but is also corrosive to exhibits. A satisfactory environment is achieved by a massive envelope of blockwork

Above left: Servicing and structure diagram.
Above: Aerial view of the museum.
Opposite: Building structure and services installation.

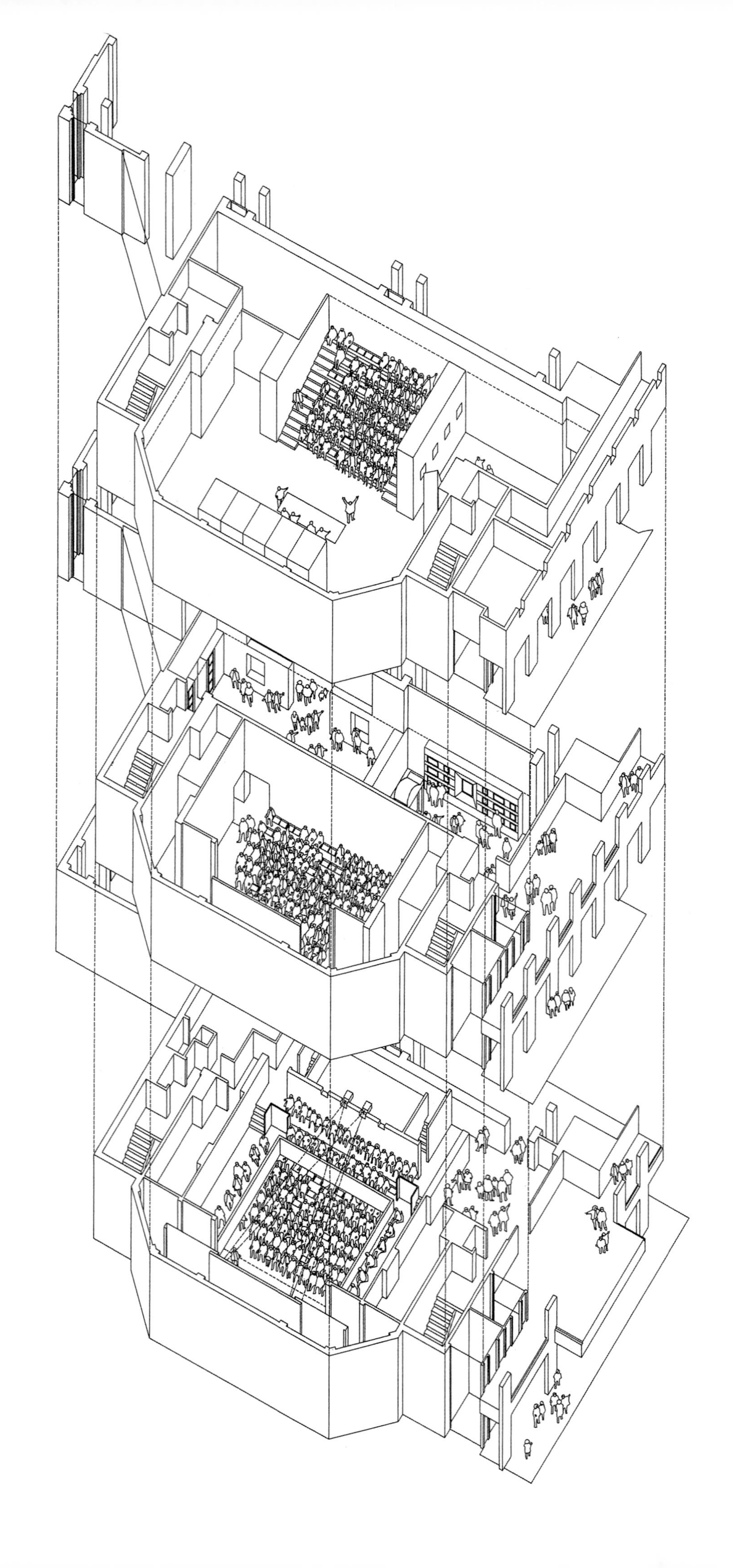

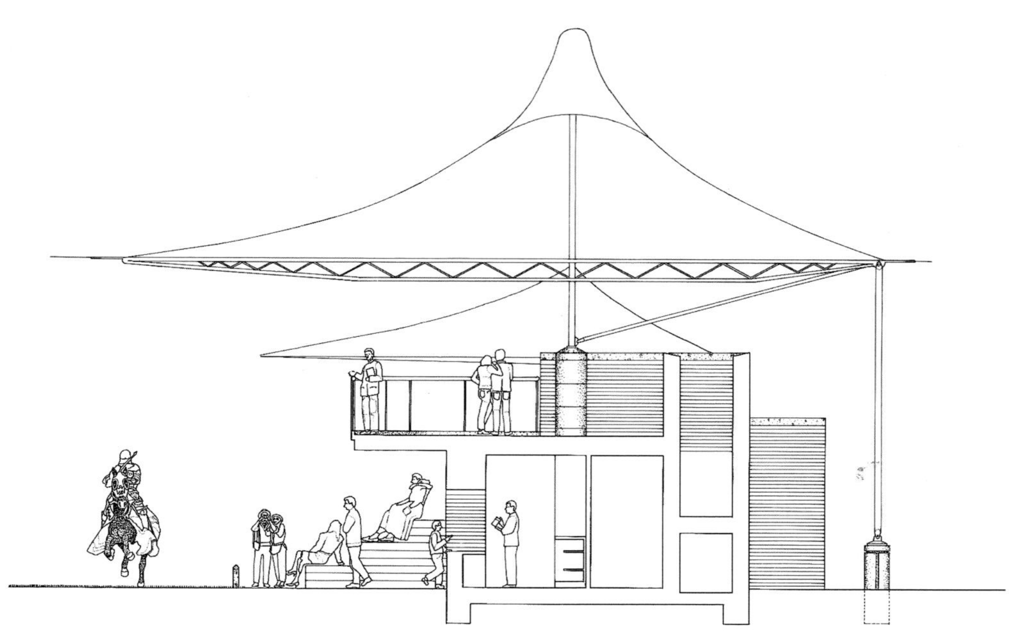

and concrete exposed so that it reacts directly with the space, punctured by very small windows in order to minimise solar gain. Evenness is so important that the building has to have the ability to be air-conditioned to guarantee ventilation, cool and heat.

The system selected was a displacement air-ventilation system. Cool air is introduced to the gallery spaces at low level and at low velocity. This cool air is then mixed with the ambient air generally by the movement of people in the space; as the air warms, from heat of lighting, other equipment, people and so on, it rises through the gallery space and is extracted at high level in the ceiling above.

For aesthetic reasons one requires that the building services and ductwork are unobtrusive and yet easily maintained. Some of the exhibits are very heavy and so the floors to the galleries have to be very strong. So effectively the main floors have twin beams and between them 'trenches' in the floor to take the ducts providing air and below a ceiling void for the extract air from the ceilings below and exposed waffle slabs to make the floors between the beams and ducts. A similar approach is used to other areas of the buildings, and the whole contrasts with the tower of the Hall of Steel with its light structure and elegant planar glazing which counterpoints this solid feeling.

Interestingly enough it all adds up to a kind of modern repeat of where the exhibits came from – the Tower of London's White Tower – a ditch around, 1.5 m-thick walls and very small slit windows. An example of the advantages of historic military engineering!

Since this piece was written, tragically Ted Happold died well before his time awaiting a heart transplant. As an engineer of astounding versatility and quality it is perhaps appropriate that the last building he and his practice should realise before his death is the Royal Armouries Museum. His parents have both made sterling contributions to his native Leeds, his father as a distinguished Professor at the University of Leeds, and his mother as a long serving member of the City Council. Ted joins that other remarkable Leeds engineer John Smeaton in the pantheon of great engineers with a contribution to the city he loved which will honour his name and consolidate his reputation.

DEREK WALKER

Above left: Section through the Tiltyard and pavilion canopy.
Above: the Dockside café elevation.
Opposite: Axonometric drawing showing the stacking of the main museum auditoria.

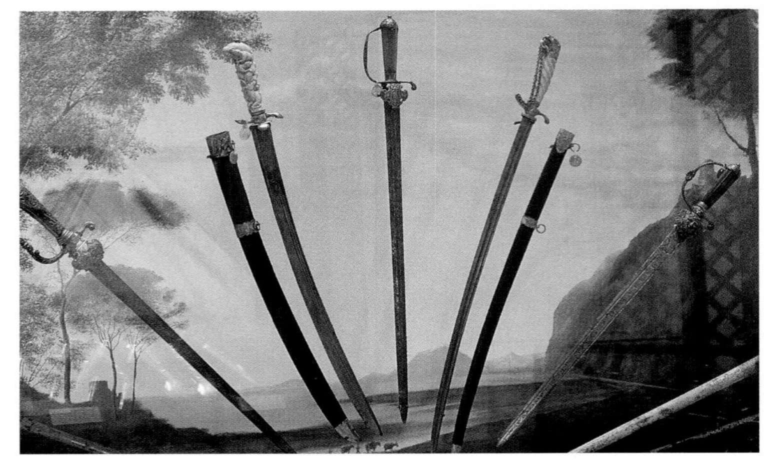

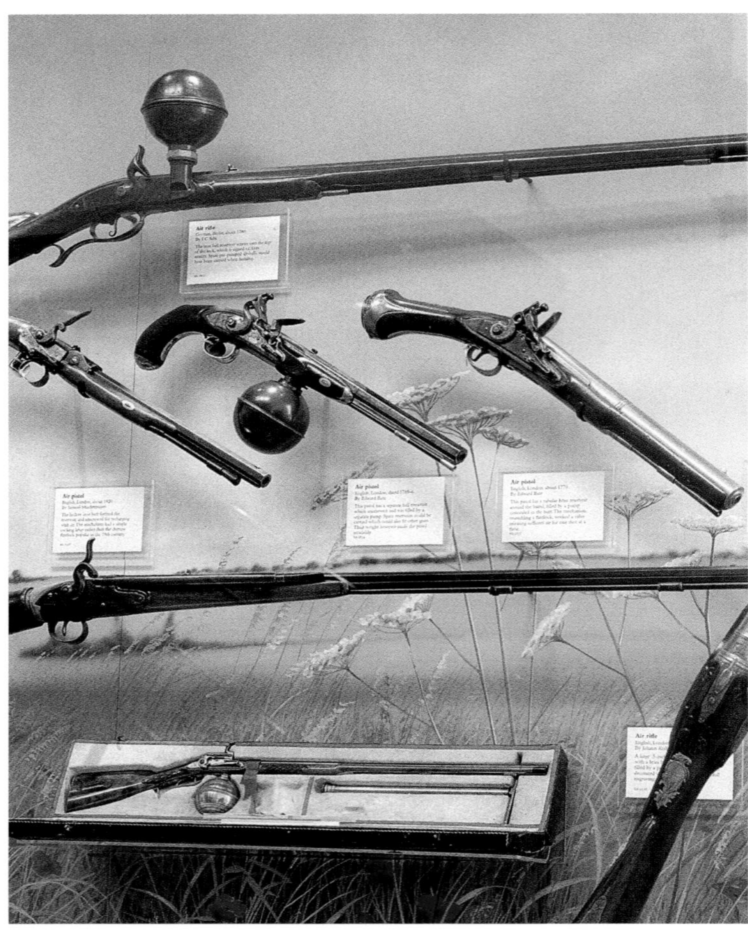

The museum interiors

DEREK WALKER

The interiors of the museum responded to three specific goals set by the Royal Armouries. First that the deliberately cool exterior should be balanced by a warm welcoming interior using a colour palette reflecting that aspiration. Second to develop display techniques which placed all objects in context and created a gallery rhythm that allowed demonstrations, films, dioramas, explanatory art and the objects to fit seamlessly into coherent and varied gallery settings. And finally to create an interior with potential for a double life as museum and community art and performance centre. That option was reflected in the general arrangement of the building and to a much lesser extent the development of the galleries themselves. The central street provides a spectacular setting for a corporate event with opportunity for music and choral singing. The temporary gallery and 250-seat cinema are linked to provide catering and conference facilities, and the main restaurant can switch with minimum disruption from a bustling museum brasserie to a formal dining room for evening functions.

The principal contractor for the interiors was the firm of Andy Thornton which has been responsible for the major gallery structures and finishes under the aegis of Heery's who acted as management contractor for the display element of the project. The ground floor and ground-floor mezzanine contain the bulk of McAlpine's interior work. The street is paved in luna pearl granite and the main structural piers and walls of the street are painted terracotta. The Street and external walls of the shop and bistro are fully glazed, and the Nelson bistro, Wellington restaurant and museum shop use a limited palette of colours – luna pearl granite, beech, stainless steel and acid-etched and diamond-cut glass. Rich colour is introduced by the goods on display, many designed specifically for the museum, or the plants, paintings and sculpture which animate the restaurant areas. The Education Department and Library use an identical double-glazed louvred partition systems specifically developed for the museum. Furniture is designed in beech and the floors are finished in beech strip or carpet, again specially designed for the museum.

Andy Thornton has been exceptionally responsive to the task of fitting out the gallery areas and have shown versatility and craftsmanship covering the many different trades and construction techniques required. They have manufactured furniture, constructed sets in GRG (glass-reinforced gypsum), GRC (glass-reinforced cement) and timber, with elements of fibrous plaster, metalwork and stained glass.

A specific design language has been developed for each gallery. In the War gallery the formal cruciform arrangement is delineated by four free-standing constructions almost two storeys in height. The circular fortification has a heavily coffered interior to accommodate the siege models, transparencies and film describing siege warfare. The roof provides the setting for a Gatling gun. The two flanking structures provide backings for the Pavia diorama and a performance area on the other side and facing into the centre of the gallery are set ten deep wall cases for selected important armours. These cases are

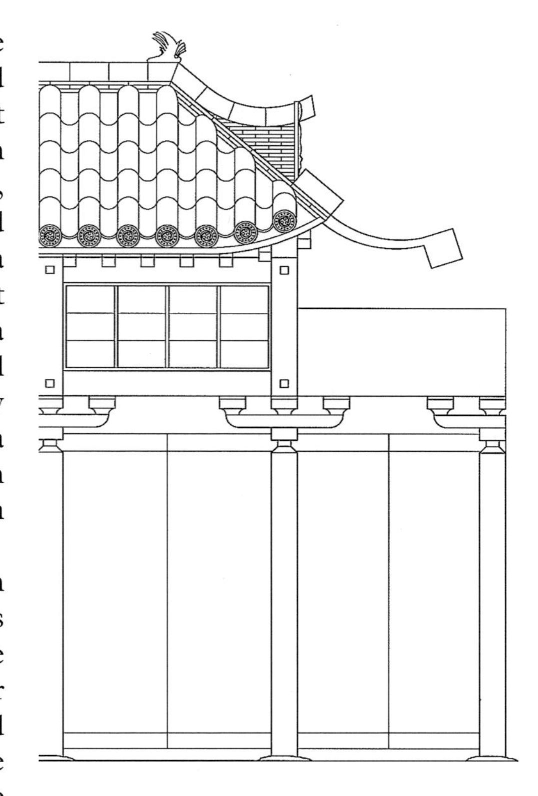

Above: Detail of the Japanese gate in the Oriental gallery.
Opposite: Top and middle, displays in the Hunting gallery; bottom left, pollaxe demonstration in the Tournament gallery; bottom right, Tudor period detailing in the Hunting gallery.

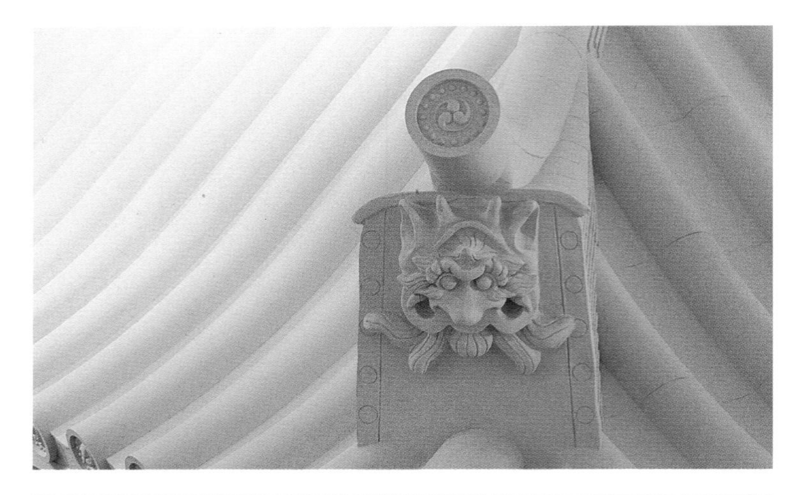

surmounted by the arms of the Board of Ordnance modelled from an original in the Tower of London and cast in GRG. The Littlecote wall completes the quartet. A ghost of the original, the decorative wall provides a setting for a formal display of a selection of the arms and armour from the Armoury of Littlecote House in Wiltshire. Centrally in the gallery Andy Thornton has built the huge cruciform set-piece in beech and slate, providing the base for four equestrian figures, four foot soldiers, and a central display of staff weapons. Three cinemas and an audio-visual room are tucked under the mezzanines at the corners of the gallery. The range of materials selected for this area is very simple in character; beech floors and furniture, glass, stainless steel, Burlington slate and specially designed carpet.

Tournament is a smaller gallery but the elements required were more complex. In the main gallery a double-fenced solid beech demonstration ring, a transparency wall and a veneered beech housing for the reproduction of a 19th-century engraving of the wonderful picture in the royal collection of the Field of Cloth of Gold. On the mezzanine there are Gothic screens, stained glass and Gothic furniture.

The Self-defence gallery was designed to threaten, with showcases arranged as a labyrinth. The gallery had modest shop-fitting requirements – coffered graphic walls, beech stands for four figure scenes by Embleton and Freeborn, and the glass screens and settings for the shooting galleries.

The two areas which gave Andy Thornton the most demanding challenge were the Oriental gallery and the Hunting gallery. The former had been designed as a series of discrete settings using the architectural language of three of the great Asian civilisations, India, China and Japan, to effect their sub-division. Three formal gateways set up the axial routes into the individual galleries and the *dojo* area. The level of detail required means that carving, modelling and laser-cutting were as much in evidence as high-quality joinery and cabinet work. The standard beech floor of the galleries also required inserts of parquet, oiled slate and decorative marble.

The Hunting gallery was developed around three octagonal sets, two roofed, one open – the first a cinema, the second a garden room for highly decorated hunting weapons and the third an Edwardian gunroom. The roofed octagons incorporate dioramas to be viewed from the gallery mezzanine. The cinema octagon is lined with a hunting fabric printed on linen. The two entry points are detailed in the Robert Smythson style and linked by a decorative cornice. The central octagon is developed as a trellised garden pavilion with murals on the inner walls in the Claude Lorrain manner; a decorative marble floor provides the base for the bronze and glass showcases. The third octagon is perhaps the most complex – a hint here of early Burges coupled with Victorian bandstand architecture. Heavily detailed with colourful entry architraves, richly stencilled internal ceiling panels, glass and oak guncases, a decorative fireplace, a small library with leather seating alcoves, and an encaustic tiled floor provide a setting for demonstration, and tales of hunting through the ages. It is apparent when visiting the museum that the interior has been the product of many contributors. McAlpine and Andy Thornton have provided the settings, but the Royal Armouries' mounting and conservation team, the showcase manufacturers, the artists and craftsmen, the hardware suppliers, the furniture manufacturers, carpet-weavers, soft-furnishing suppliers and above all the lighting consultants and suppliers have created rich and complex settings to explore a subject that encapsulates our history and gives pointers to our rather uncertain future.

Above: Design drawing for the Gothic screen in the Tournament gallery.
Opposite: Top left, detail of the Japanese gate in the Oriental gallery; top right, Japanese *yabusame* archer lent by the Nikko Toshogu Shrine in the Oriental gallery; centre left, the *Tree of Honour* in the Tournament gallery; centre right, *An ugly customer*, the tiger-hunt tableau; bottom left, replica of the arms of the Board of Ordnance; bottom right, the cruciform display in the War gallery.
Following pages: Shopfitting in the museum. The work of Andy Thornton, architectural drawings and completed work.

Cinema

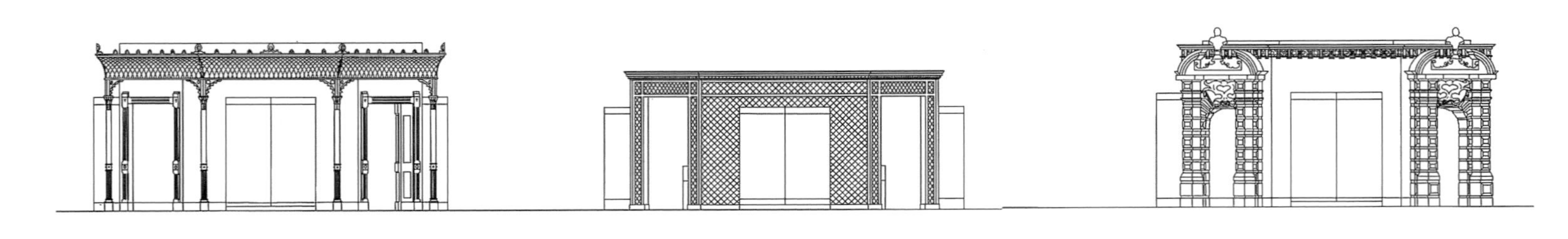

POLICE

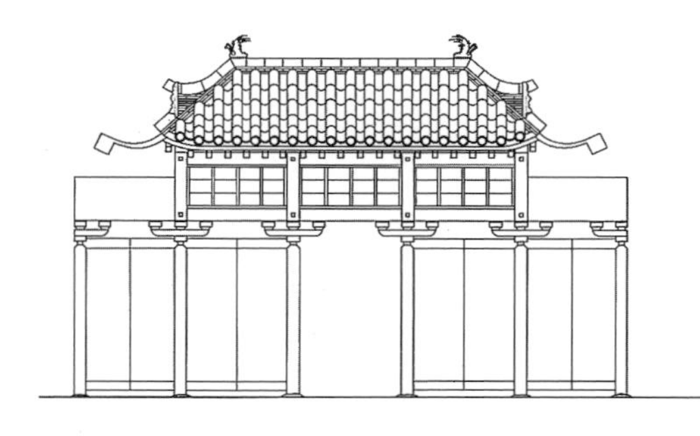

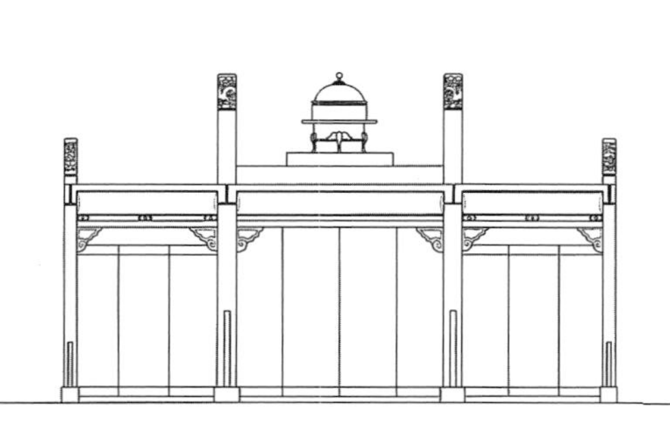

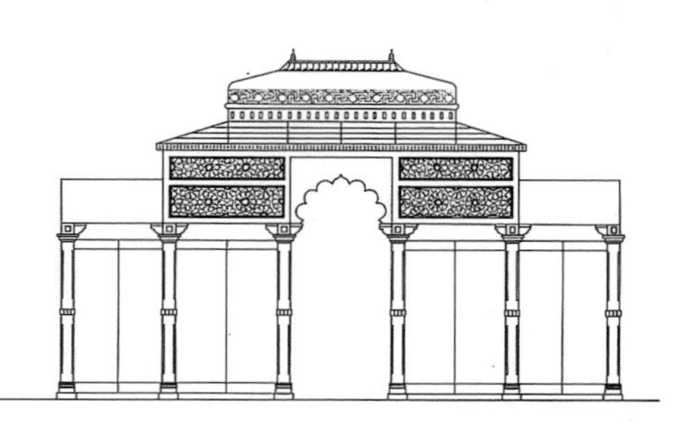

OPENED BY
HM
THE QUEEN
1996
OPENED BY
HM
THE QUEEN
1996

The museum complete

STEPHEN GARDINER

It isn't easy to pin down the quality which best expresses the pleasure given by a good building. I remember a friend on the *Observer* putting it well when he said, 'Most of the time we are surrounded with chaos. Then you can suddenly turn and be confronted by an 18th-century terrace – and sanity. It may be derelict, but it is still sanity'.

He was of course referring to the pleasures of an aesthetic order, to the importance of achieving a calm and a reticence in design, so generally absent from the architectural scene today. The element of surprise comes into the matter too: the rarity of being given pleasure is a telling factor, as indeed is the effect of contrast. You experience both on arrival at the Royal Armouries Museum. You have driven from the station and perhaps enjoyed picking your way through the centre of red-brick 19th-century Leeds, been utterly shocked by the ludicrously ugly new office building at Quarry Hill, have then negotiated traffic jams lined with the remnants of industrial sheds on the other side of the river Aire before suddenly turning left, getting your first complete view of the museum's south front – and there you have it, a picture of sanity. A rush of thoughts momentarily enters your head (confused attempts to analyse what you see architecturally). Really, I suppose, your main feelings are of relief.

Here is a work that, although huge, doesn't impose itself upon you; is simple, straightforward and wonderfully unaffected, yet which manages to convey, through the personality of its architect, Derek Walker, that most mysterious of all qualities, humanity. At first glance, the details of this remarkable building – where, for instance, the entrance is, what some strange windows mean – pass you by. To start with, it's the massing that counts, and if there is an aesthetic point here that's at once striking, it is the strength with which this grips the eye: surroundings are edited out, abandoned structures to the left across the Clarence Dock fail to register, and even the fine warehouses over the river to the right are reduced to a pink blur as the enormous, flat, gunmetal grey of the brick facade, interleaved with slices of glass and strips of stone, arrests the attention. This, for now, is what concerns you.

It's an interesting point. For another example, take St Paul's: I've often noticed that Christopher Wren's building is so powerful that its depressing commercial neighbours make scarcely any impact; one's gaze is focused solely on the cathedral, so enfeebled are they by its presence. Similarly with the museum: in this case, with the building anchored to the apex of a fan-shaped site, with the river, its racing weir, lock and dock surrounding it on two sides, the rest of the land (14 acres in all) acts as the approach that converges on the entrance with lines of trees and gardens. With the long wall of the Tiltyard on the right, the combined effect of all these elements gives the approach a force, pointing the entrance out. The wide brick walkway, running beside the entrance road, leads straight to the tall glass wall above it, and then continues right through the building, ending with a climax like a clash of cymbals, the Hall of Steel. The focus, from the delicate

Above: Top, design discussion in the architect's office between the Master of the Armouries and David Reddick of Derek Walker Associates; bottom, castles and sieges display in the War gallery.
Opposite: Main south entrance to the museum.

preliminaries of the approach to the mounting suspense as the interior is penetrated, is total.

An entrance flawlessly resolving the relationship of internal and external space, and which by some deft piece of sleight-of-hand can make barriers apparently vanish, is one of the secrets central to any good building, particularly when it is of the important public kind, as here. Yet this is what Derek Walker and his team have achieved, and they have done so by introducing an immense volume of space that runs through the museum's length and height. It is called the Street and has the practical value of connecting the main south and west entrances and leads to the knot of public vertical circulation elements, the bank of glazed lifts and the grand staircase winding round the core of the Hall of Steel. The Street provides the focus of all circulation activity, and this is highly important: it means that visitors can locate their position wherever they are, the Street being the connection to every part of the building. You can't miss it: from the white interior of the galleries, education areas, restaurants and the rest, the main structure of the Street is terracotta-coloured so that there is absolutely no possibility of getting lost, or losing a sense of direction, or feeling oppressed by dozens of galleries leading on and on without a break in sequence, endlessly. This is a great contrast to many museums, even some major ones, which seem to have no centre, and with their dull linoleum shine tend to bore and disorientate school children, so putting them off a fascinating source of knowledge during their most impressionable years.

From a planning point of view therefore, the Street, with a café break next to the staircase and lifts at all levels, is an excellent innovation. For all that, it has its origins in Leeds, in the superb arcades which many regard as the finest examples of their kind in the country. As Walker, a Yorkshireman, says, he grew up with them, and his Street is in fact a dramatisation of the form. It could be said that was part of his psyche, a personal source of inspiration which found the perfect application at the museum in this important industrial city of the Victorian era. Its employment was a daring means of meeting the requirements of the architect's brief, namely, that of a 'radiating' plan with a central circulation spine from which galleries could be visited in any order. It's doubtful if anyone reading this plain statement could have believed that an architect would, having accepted this for what it said, and turn words like 'spine' and 'circulation' into nothing less than an architectural spectacular.

Walker, however, saw other possibilities in it. For one thing, the Street brought a breathing space to the centre of a dense arrangement of exhibits, a place where the visitor can, if you like, sit over a coffee in one of the cafés overlooking the dockside and think about it all, or enjoy – yes, and this is important too – the architecture as an exhibit in itself: the glass-sided bridges (transparency means that obstructions to the space are minimal) connecting both parts of the museum at the five upper levels, the lightness of the roof structure, the abstract composition of the openings running up the Street's facades – together display modern architecture at its very best. From one of the bridges too, you have the full effect of the Street vanishing away in sharp perspective, through the glass wall of the entrance and on into the distance as the promenade, the idea that ties inside and out in a tight grip with one another, the space outside flowing inside.

It is a great effect, bringing to mind the broader meaning of space in building, and, in addition, what the loss of space has done to damage architecture at the commercial end of development schemes. It is a fact that space, when considered in volumes of it (a very different matter from measuring it in terms of areas), separates true architecture from the mundane, the run-of-the-mill; it is the factor that is so difficult to justify in material terms, but which is vitally important in aesthetic ones, the essential element that introduces a sense of calm and relaxation to a building. Architecture today is just as dependent upon generous space as any other style (*Greek, Chinese, Palladian, Georgian*), and the concentration of it in the museum's Street and Hall of Steel demonstrates why: space is architecture – like art it is an experience, and, like art too, incapable of explanation.

There are many beautiful moments, images and associations in this very large and unusual building. I think, for instance, of a glancing view of the riverside's stone edge through a slip of glass between the end of the Street and the hefty granite podium of the Hall of Steel – just a glimpse, but enough to feel the sensual effect of one choice material lodged next to another. I think of the balcony around the War gallery where the structure does the work and where I felt I was in a movie of shifting white backgrounds, cut to reveal remarkable life-size likenesses of horses in battle dress and men in Gothic armour; and of the Japanese, Chinese and Indian entrances in the Oriental section, mock-ups in off-white fibrous plaster so subdued (Walker describes them as 'ghosts') that they can double as frames for the glass cases of exhibits. This is display at its most urbane, laid-back: no feeling of pressure, no overcrowding, nothing heavy – the seamless design of the interior architecture carries on through the exhibition spaces: the signature is the same, throughout, maintaining unity and invention.

So far as ideas go, some of the best on the education side are in the demonstration areas in the War, Oriental and Tournament galleries where there are performances by experts (who are also actors) skilled in handling weapons, tilting and foot combat who re-enact wide-ranging historical events to bring them to life; they may be to do with the arrowstorm of Agincourt, the American Civil War or the battles of World War One. At the same time, there are demonstrations outside, overlooking the dock, and in the Tiltyard where, from bleacher seating, audiences watch demonstrations with horses, dogs and birds of prey. Everywhere, in fact, there is activity and movement, changing scenes as in a theatre, all of which, stimulating, vivid and certainly popular, are designed to excite the imagination.

Then, there is the sequence of octagonal sets for the Hunting gallery which are among the wittiest of the display concepts and, in the use of the roof of one as a snow-scene for an Alpine hunt, the cleverest. But for display at its most magnificent and brilliant, the Hall of Steel is of course unique. As the climax at the apex of both fan-shaped site and the building, this is how it should be, a dramatic finale that is entirely to do with the interesting way in which an octagonal form has been used to exhibit a mass of weapons and armour in a myriad of glittering patterns. This is the internal picture: around it winds the staircase which is clothed externally with steel and glass, finishing at the top with a cupola reached by an intricate, transparent little staircase. Yet the multitude of pistols, swords, spears and the rest, beautifully though they are arranged, remind one of the other side of the story – the sheer horror and nightmare of war, killing, violence of all kinds, from hunting wild boar in the heyday of the Indian Raj to 20,000,000 dead in the First World War and 50,000,000 in the Second.

The 20th century may well be remembered as the age of Waste – wasted

Above: Top, the foot combat ring in theTournament gallery; bottom, punt-gunning tableau in the Hunting gallery. *Opposite:* Top, the museum from the river Aire; bottom, the chamois-hunt tableau in the Hunting gallery.

opportunities, resources, lives. And it is the effort given to portraying this other side of the story that is as conscientiously and memorably treated as any other part of this magnificent museum. As Walker says, he was haunted by thoughts of the suffering inflicted on man by man when he was involved with the brief-writing and conceptual design phase, and how this could be exposed through the building and its display. Many ways of doing so have been adopted, quite apart from relying on reactions to mock-ups of men in combat, hunting for 'sport', an elephant attacked by a tiger, a huge model of the battle of Waterloo (made shortly after it) and so forth. One, of course, is with the use of audio-visual aids: I found myself transfixed by rushes from First World War films, by the news that 20,000 men died in a few hours in the Somme offensive (which achieved nothing), by the squalor of the trenches, the terror of 'going over the top', the shell-shocked victims (making me think immediately of the 300 soldiers executed for 'cowardice') – all this, in the context of the display of superbly crafted guns and bayonets in show cases around, had an indescribable poignancy, causing irrepressible sensations of anger and disgust.

And then there was that other exceptional use of film in a cinema off the War gallery. First you are entertained by streams of pictures displaying pomp and circumstance, victory marches, flags waving, gold braid, bands playing, crowds cheering, brilliant colours, ranks of soldiers saluting – this is the glamorised war 'commercial', the romantic gloss of the propaganda-aided picture. The film in the next-door cinema blows that to smithereens in seconds: here's the truth, the nightmare, cities bombed flat, the world in flames, an extraordinary montage of destruction on the grandest scale, vividly seen and directed, and terrifyingly real. For Walker, however, this wasn't enough: he wanted the theme to run on through the architecture itself, he felt the need to express something of the meaning of war with it, investing it 'with an element of danger and menace'. This could possibly explain one's reaction on first seeing it. Here I thought, was an immensely formidable building, a fortress of a place, a kind of 'castle'.

There are plain associations with the castle wall – solid ramparts, thick and impenetrable, 'arrow-slot' windows and lookouts. One's not imagining things – even the strip of glass at the entrance, 30 m high, has an eerie memory of the 'drawbridge'. And then there's the Hall of Steel, tall, octagonal, shimmering with glass and stainless steel supports upon its granite base, which had for me the oddest of recalls – Yorkshire's bare, 12th-century keep at Conisbrough Castle, a nice thought, particularly when it's reinforced by a flashback to the 'moat' in the surrounding water of the river and dock. The source of inspiration lay with the museum's function and with the setting, and in the way the building could be seen as a portrait of people and the place.

And it's a complete portrait, a reason why it remains as firm as a tablet in the memory. Walker takes his architecture right to the water's edge, to the powerful, muscular shape of the lock's island and giant gritstone blocks of Clarence Dock from which the dark strength and huge scale of the museum sprang, using the stone from a demolished bridge to continue the sculptural forms. There are no loose ends.

Credit for this lies with a strong design team, with the extraordinary expertise of model makers of horses, tigers and other animals, with the brilliance of the graphics by Brian Tattersfield of Minale Tattersfield, and with the indefatigable support and positive involvement of Guy Wilson.

Above: Top, detail Hall of Steel interior; bottom, detail of the south entrance.
Opposite: Night and dusk shots of the museum from the entrance to Clarence Dock.
Following pages: Views of the completed museum.

The museum showcases

DEREK WALKER

Dealing with a collection of this variety of type and scale with so many different technical and climatic requirements was a formidable task. The collection required over 200 showcases and it became clear in the design process that one specialist group was going to be hard pressed to provide the complete package. Showcase manufacturers world-wide seem to fall into two categories – those with adaptable standard systems that can be customised to a degree to suit specific design criteria, and those with a more inventive engineering base specialising in individual solutions. Fortunately the two most competitive and appropriate companies on our tender list each represented one of these approaches.

The most interesting starting point for the designers was Click's award-winning Inca system originally developed in the late eighties. Inca is a silicon-sealed glass box system in three variants. Laminated glass up to 18 mm thick can be used to glaze very tall areas. A sophisticated environmental control system is incorporated together with Click's own Flex fibre-optic system. In order to accommodate the latest type of sealing materials and to allow specific design features developed by the architects, Click have taken the opportunity to further refine and extend Inca into version IV. This system allows multiple side-by-side door openings with aggregate spans up to five metres and fully integrated fibre-optic and low voltage lighting. This development which demanded seventeen new extrusions as well as dozens of small standard parts has been designed and produced in four months in parallel with the room-sized street cases designed with the architects.

Goppion, a Milan-based company offered a complementary experience. I had been particularly impressed with their work in a number of Italian museums. A massive hydraulic jacking device developed for a case housing the reliquary in the Cathedral of Orvieto and the protection of the statue of David in the Galleria dell'Accademia in Florence were both brilliant engineering solutions, as were their horizontal cabinets supported by a multifunctional handrail containing lighting equipment and the thermo-hygrometer data survey apparatus at the Castelgrande Museum in Bellinzona. Closer to home they were also awarded the prestigious contract to provide showcases for the Jewel House in the Tower of London. Applied research and engineering are central to Goppion Laboratorio's activities. They display a level of craft skill that mirrors the most sophisticated innovations of Italian product design.

For the Waterloo model the seven-metre-long case required total access. We needed hydraulic cases for three galleries, and glass cases cut on the diagonal with a separating mechanism to allow placement of full armours with unimpeded access. Goppion have provided opening systems, normal or motorised, mitred glass jointing systems, passive and active security and air-filtering systems as standard components for the cases they have developed with the architect for the Leeds museum. They have done this at a level of craftsmanship in keeping with the most formidable pieces in the collection.

Above: Top, Derek Walker and Sandro Goppion in Goppion's Milan factory; bottom, a Goppion case in the Tournament gallery.
Opposite: Top, the work of Goppion: left, a screen for the statue of David in Florence; right, showcase for the cathedral of Orvieto; bottom, room-sized case by Click for the Oriental gallery.

The audio-visual hardware

DEREK WALKER

Simon Harris and his company AVE have provided the audio-visual package for the museum. The main auditorium seating 250 people is designed to present major feature films, lectures, recitals and poetry readings. Equipment is mainly housed in the projection room and consists of state of the art projectors and sound systems. The cinema has also been equipped with a high quality video projector mounted on a scissors lift to allow it to be retractable when not in use.

Both the Hunting gallery and War gallery have introductory cinemas using special long-throw LCD video projectors; video projectors are also used in three small cinemas under the mezzanine of the War gallery.

The Newsroom contains technical equipment to allow several different studio formats. Satellite dishes and receivers enable pictures from around the world to be shown on wallmounted monitors in the entrance area and on a large 15-screen video wall at the rear of the main studio directly opposite the spectator seating area. A lighting bank over the central studio area allows options for panel debate and presentation which can be transferred to the video wall from the glass-fronted video editing suite in the Newsroom which also works the information monitors in the Street.

The films and sound programmes in the galleries are driven by laser disks and laser disk players. The players together with all other technical equipment are housed in a central racks room. Control systems, audio amplifiers and the players run the displays automatically. The area is fully air-conditioned and has a maintenance capability in an adjacent workshop.

The architects have designed a special bronze-finished stalk monitor-housing for the majority of the smaller 15" screens in the galleries, power, video and audio cables being routed up them from underfloor conduits.

Four additional areas of the War gallery also required detailed AVE input. The *Theatre of war* demonstration area is equipped for performance with microphones and a number of lighting set changes. The *Sights and sounds of war* utilises ceiling mounted projectors with a synchronised soundtrack.

The Waterloo model has two monitors suspended over the model showing extracts from the feature film and description of the battle; the sound sequence triggers lighting effects on the model highlighting the areas of action.

The wargames area on the mezzanine uses a camera to relay the wargame being enacted and a second lipstick camera for close-up work; the game enactment and appropriate back-up material is shown on the two screens placed behind the wargaming table.

Other areas are also linked back to the racks room and monitors and cameras reflect detail of the work being carried out. The cable link from the Tiltyard monitors and transmits events in the Tiltyard.

Finally AVE have developed with the Royal Armouries and their architects a laser shooting gallery. Themed to achieve maximum authenticity and programmed as a police training range, this introduces the visitor to the problems of split-second decision-making and target recognition which makes the job of the policeman armed with firearms so difficult.

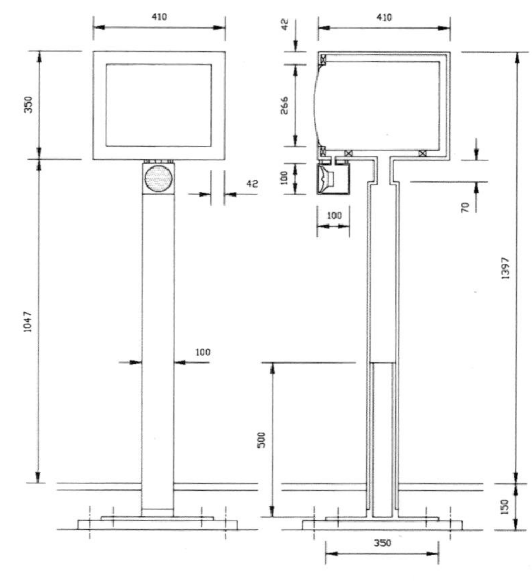

Above: Top, one of the interactive computers in the museum; bottom, monitor-housing designed by Derek Walker Associates. *Opposite:* Top, general view of the Tournament gallery; bottom left, pig-sticking tableau in the Hunting gallery; bottom right, a vision of war in space in the War gallery.

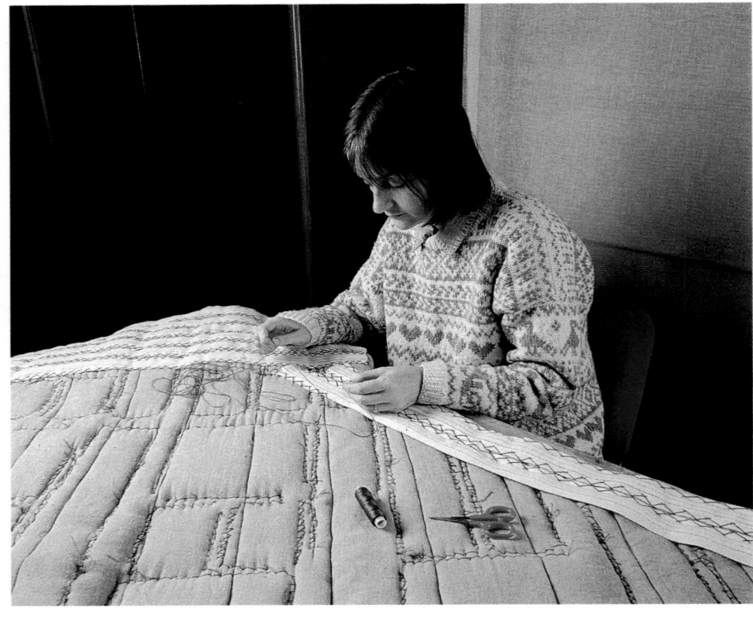

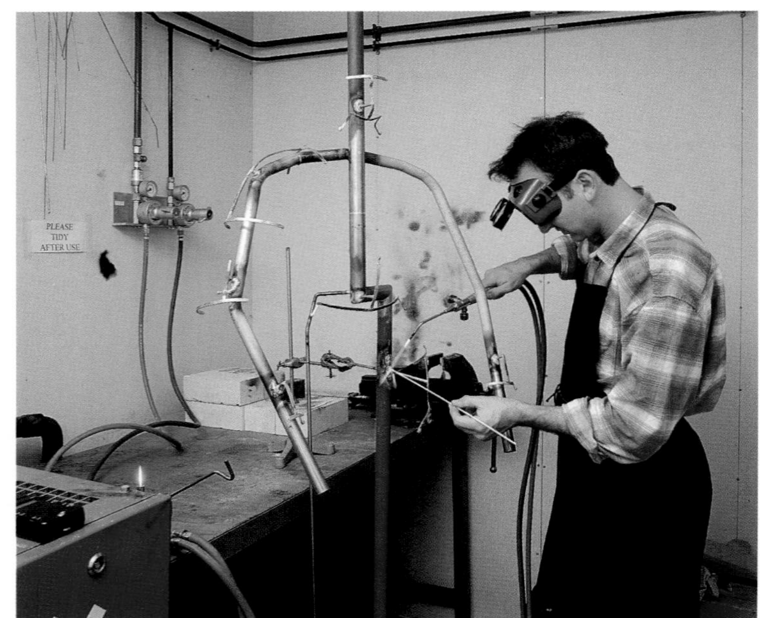
PLEASE
TIDY
AFTER USE

The conservation process

GUY WILSON

To display thousands of objects from any collection that have either never been displayed before, or at least have not been displayed for many years, imposes a heavy burden of conservation. They all have to be selected, cleaned, and many have to be restored. This has been the fundamental task of our team of conservators in this as in any project. But in making an entirely new museum there are many other jobs to be done. Our conservators have had to work closely with the design team to ensure that the new museum building and its new displays met the increasingly stringent criteria for environmental conditions and use of inert and safe materials that we as all museums now have to impose. They have had to work with curators and designers in creating the object displays and have been responsible for making all the individually hand-crafted mounts and brackets required safely and elegantly to display thousands of precious objects. With our registrars they have had to organise the packing in London, safe transport to Leeds, and unpacking of the objects in the collection, whether they were destined for display or the reserve collections. They have then had to organise the safe installation of all the displays to the tightest of timescales, and to liaise with all the other craftsmen and consultants to ensure that all came together at the right time.

It was a colossal task, and, as with the work of the curators, involved tracking and organising the work to be done on our computerised collections management system. Once a case layout had been agreed in the Tower the objects were sent back to store or display there to await packing, the position of each in Leeds recorded on computer so that, when the time came to pack them, items from around the museum that were to be displayed together in Leeds could be quickly gathered and packed together. Meanwhile, the mounts for each individual object were numbered, recorded and packed, display case by display case, so that they could be made readily available in Leeds when required. When all these packing cases and crates arrived in Leeds their individual numbers and locations had to be recorded so that when particular objects or brackets were required for mounting they could be swiftly found and efficiently delivered to the two and three person teams undertaking the display mounting.

Meanwhile the basic, painstaking, and highly skilled work of conservation had to proceed, even over the period of packing and moving the conservation laboratories and working areas from London to Leeds. Major work was required, especially on the Oriental arms and armour with its preponderance of fragile fabrics, before the collection could be safely moved, let alone be displayed in a manner to do its quality justice. Major improvements in the condition of many of our fabric armours were achieved in this frantic period in less than ideal working conditions, and a wholescale renovation of our unique elephant armour was completed. That this and all the other work was achieved is a tribute to the professional skill and dedication of our small team of conservators and to the additional craftsmen and technicians whom we employed for the duration of the project to work with them.

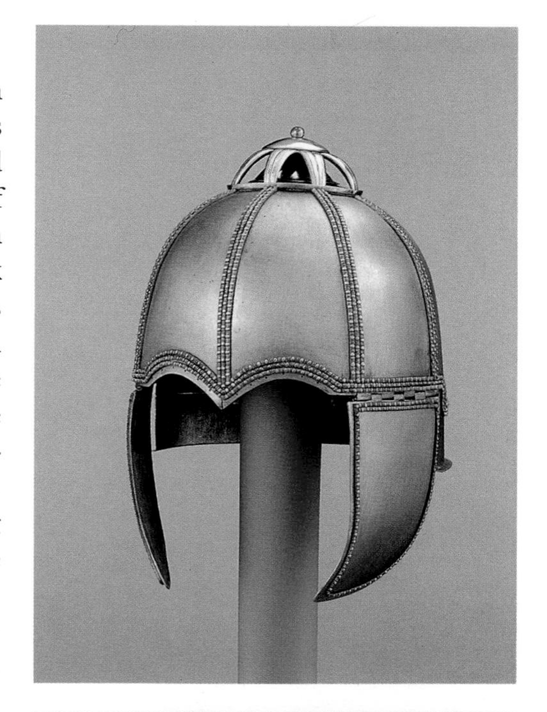

Above: Replicas of the Sardis helmet, Lydian, 5th century BC, and the Sutton Hoo helmet, Anglo-Saxon, 7th century AD, reproduced by the Royal Armouries.
Opposite: The conservators at work – object preparation and packing.
Following pages: Details of completed displays and objects on the Oriental gallery; design sketches and display mock-ups.

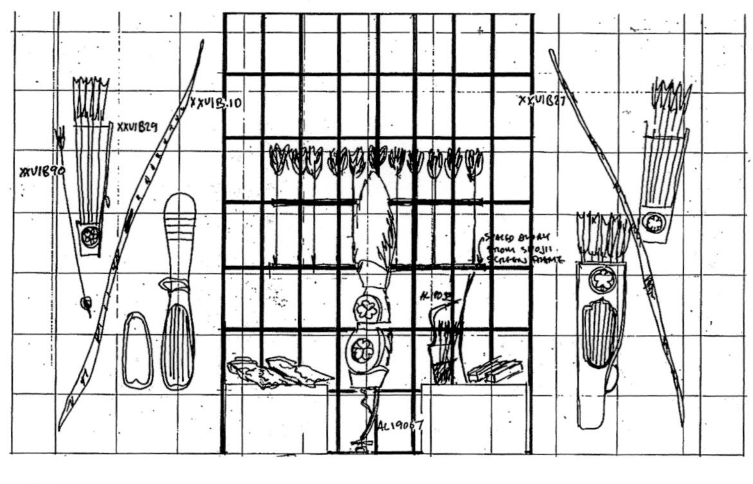

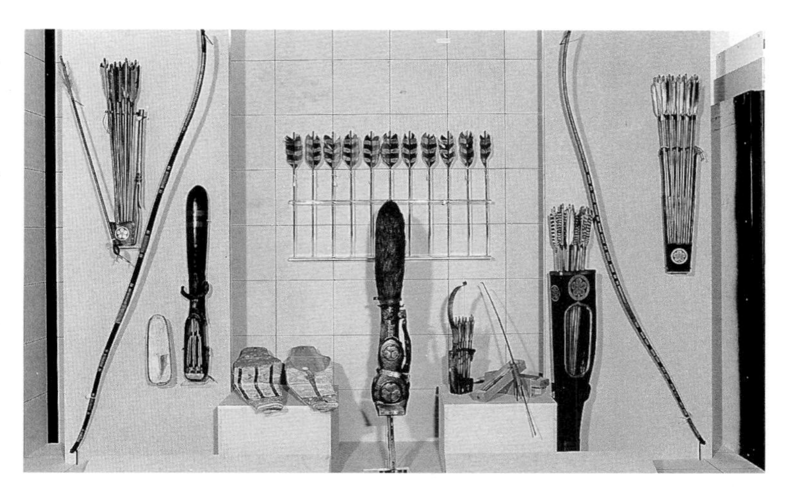

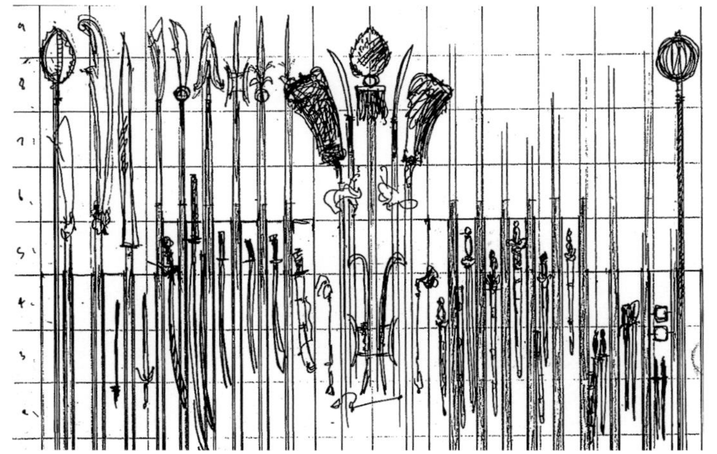

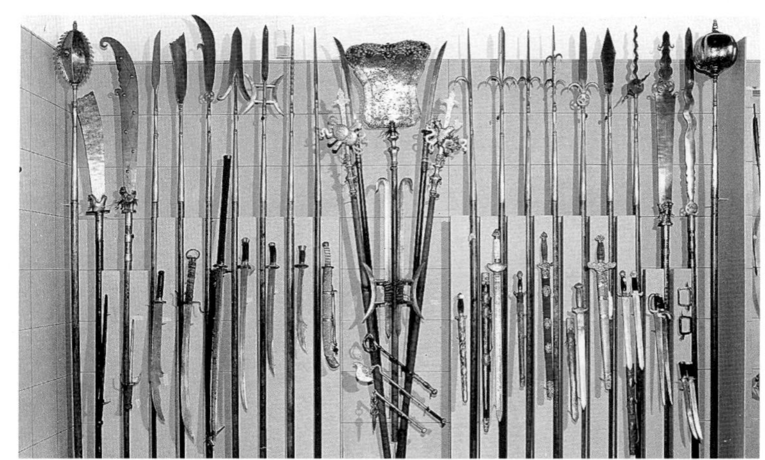

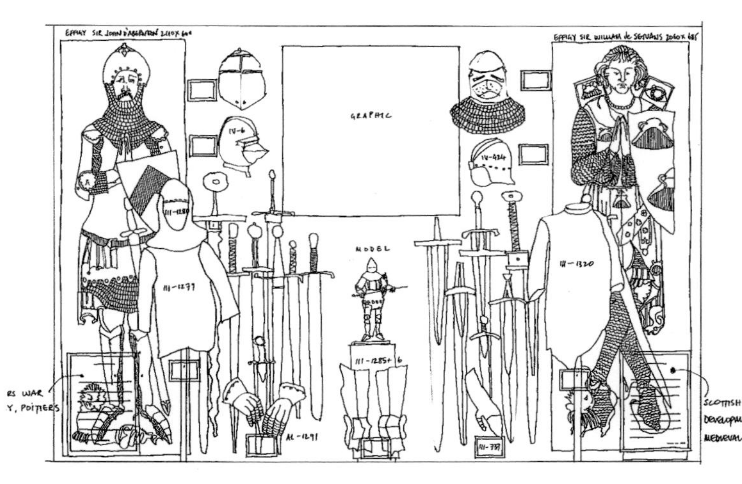

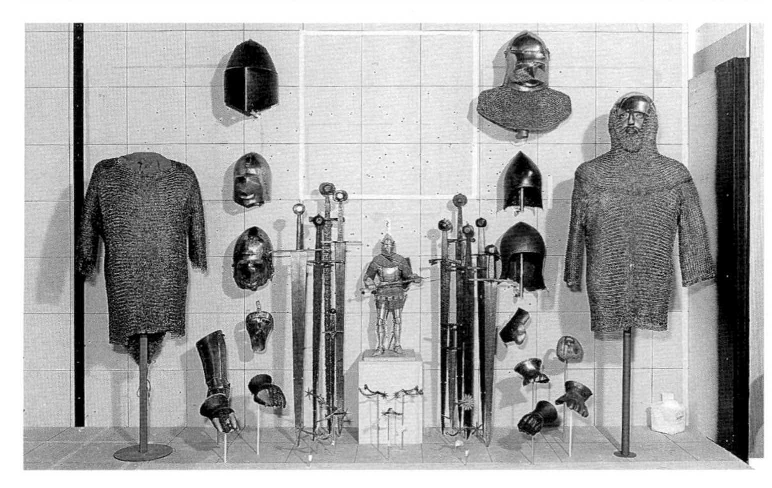

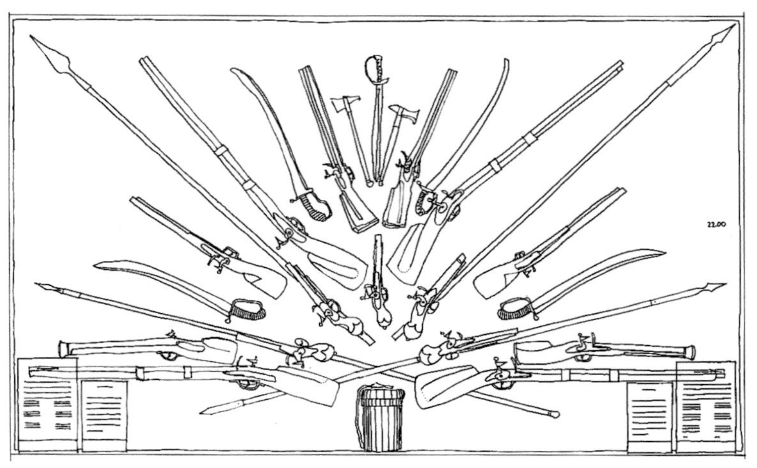

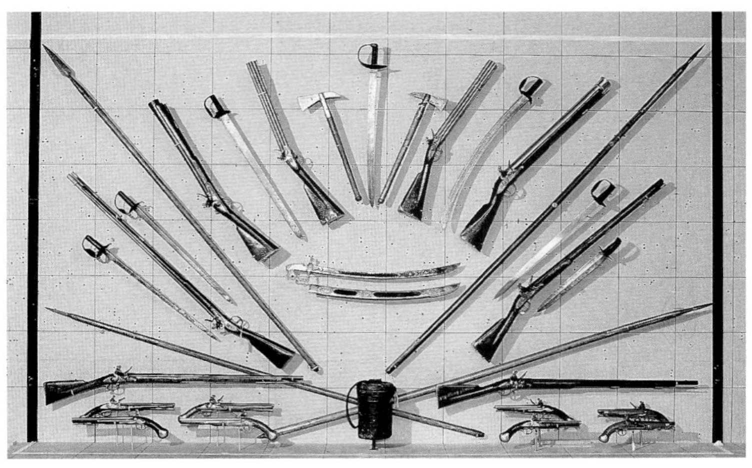

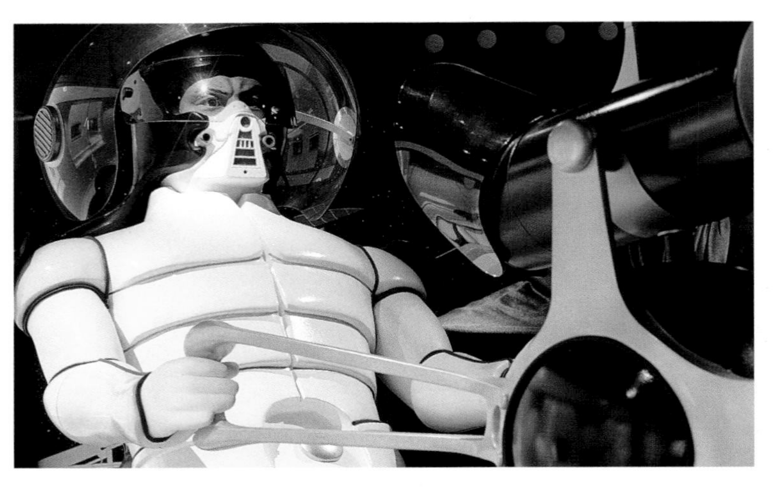

The artists and craftsmen

DEREK WALKER

In some ways, our decision to use artists and craftsmen in the museum was not universally popular in museum circles. The desire to make a museum more accessible and intelligible to a wider public meant the introduction of film, demonstration, and interactive elements, and the wide use of explanatory text and visual imagery, all of which, some feared, might result in the objects themselves being swamped by contemporary interlopers that could detract from the collection. If this wasn't enough, artists and craftsmen were also being asked to prepare models, animals, figures and constructions which further muddied the waters of aesthetic appreciation. Nothing was further from our minds as we sought to bring together elements that brought into focus the past and the future in order positively to enhance the objects and make the experience more vivid to the visitor.

The four major contributors to this section of the display were Bill Gordon, David Hayes, Gerry Embleton and Kit Freeborn. Each operated a small studio with a dedicated team capable of producing exquisite work at a variety of scales, some rather more focused and specialised than others, but between them providing craft skills that covered the widest possible spectrum of display requirements. I first saw Kit Freeborn's work in the Los Angeles Holocaust Museum – a superb Berlin Café scene of the thirties modelled at two-thirds life-size. This presentation set the scene in such a seductive and normal manner that the sinister and degrading character of the death camps that followed were etched in even more horrifying relief as a result. This talent for accurate and realistic representation is matched by Gerry Embleton who has tended to specialise in military subjects. A keen student of medieval history and an illustrator of considerable talent, his work is well known to museums throughout Europe. Within the museum he has straddled the centuries with pieces for Towton and Pavia, World War I and tomorrow's next bloody tragedy, wherever it may be. He has been ably assisted by Keith Bartlett who provided the costumes and uniforms. Paradoxically David Hayes has been that missing ingredient that most projects of this kind often fail to find – a modest man with an extraordinary talent. A near-perfect rhinoceros spread across the Sunday times magazine led us to his studio in Hornsey and prefaced his involvement in the project. A different approach was taken for the equestrian figures in the Oriental gallery, where H & H Sculptors modelled the horses. Bill Gordon and his partner Brian Archer are both long-time collaborators with my practice. Architectural modelmakers of remarkable versatility, they made many of the earlier study models for the museum. Since then their scope on the project has escalated and they have made remarkable limewood models of castles, fortifications and siege weapons as well as a variety of other larger elements for the museum from the organic, a puntgunning tableau and a chamois hunt, to the eclectic, a Japanese teahouse, a medieval shooting gallery, a large Pollock theatre to house a vidiwall and the Tents and a Tree of Honour for the Tournament gallery. Throughout, the craftsmen have been inspired by the quality of the collection. We have been fortunate to collaborate with such a meticulous and dedicated group.

Above: Top, model of a city fortified by Vauban; bottom, *A vision of war in space* by David Reddick.
Opposite: The use of sculptural figures in the museum displays by David Hayes, Bill Gordon and Gerry Embleton.

SOIT QUI MAL Y PENSE
DIEU ET. MON DROIT

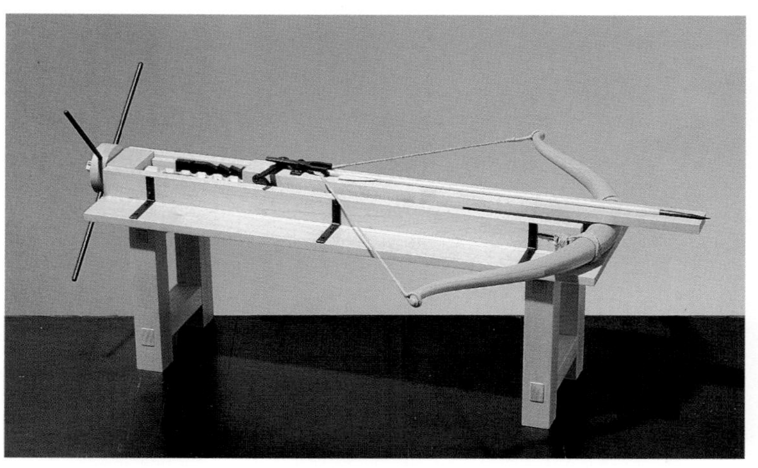

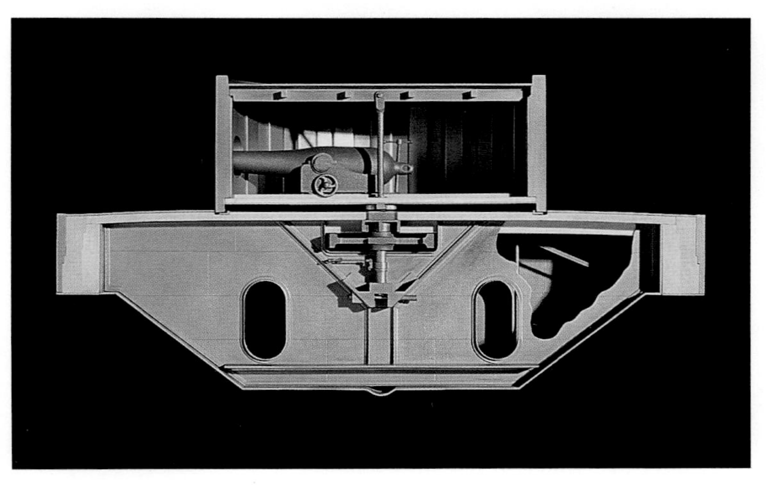

Bill Gordon
Gordon Models' versatility is amply illustrated in the preceding pages. They have worked on the project since its inception, first producing small-scale models of the building, the interiors and display. Their commissions in the building include a wide variety of limewood and metal models, full-size room-sets culminating in their largest installation, the medieval shooting gallery, designed by Brian Tattersfield and Derek Walker, which tested Gordon's craft skills to the full. High-quality joinery, theatrical lighting, support mechanisms in metal, moving parts, scenic painting, engineered figures with hydraulic re-sets, even the crossbow bolts had to be adapted quite radically to avoid bounce on impact. This small section of the museum exemplified the real focus of inventive innovation shared by the designers and many of the craftsmen.

Above and left: the work of Gordon Models for the War gallery.
Opposite: Gordon Models workshop, sets and models in preparation.

These two pages represent the collective efforts of the design team to maximise the impact of great set-pieces within the gallery.

Left: In the comparative tranquillity of the architect's office, Guy Wilson, Brian Tattersfield, Julian Baker and Derek Walker discuss the maquettes prepared by David Hayes for the two major pieces placed outside the Hunting gallery.
Above left: The development of the pig-sticking set is shown in development.
Above right: The tiger hunt concept by Elizabeth Bury, animals by David Hayes, figures by Gerry Embleton and Keith Bartlett, is discussed as the scene develops by the authors. The barn in Gloucestershire provided David Hayes with the studio space required for the major set-pieces.
Opposite: Top, the rhinoceros being coloured and prepared for its incorporation into the African hunting scene in one of the Street cases. Bottom, Gerry Embleton's first sketch for the diorama of Pavia, a set-piece that involved most of the creative team, client, architects, Bill Gordon, Elizabeth Bury, David Hayes and Gerry Embleton. It is hoped that the scholarship of the Royal Armouries and the craftsmanship of the artists has captured the essence of Pavia, one of the first battles in which handguns played a crucial part.

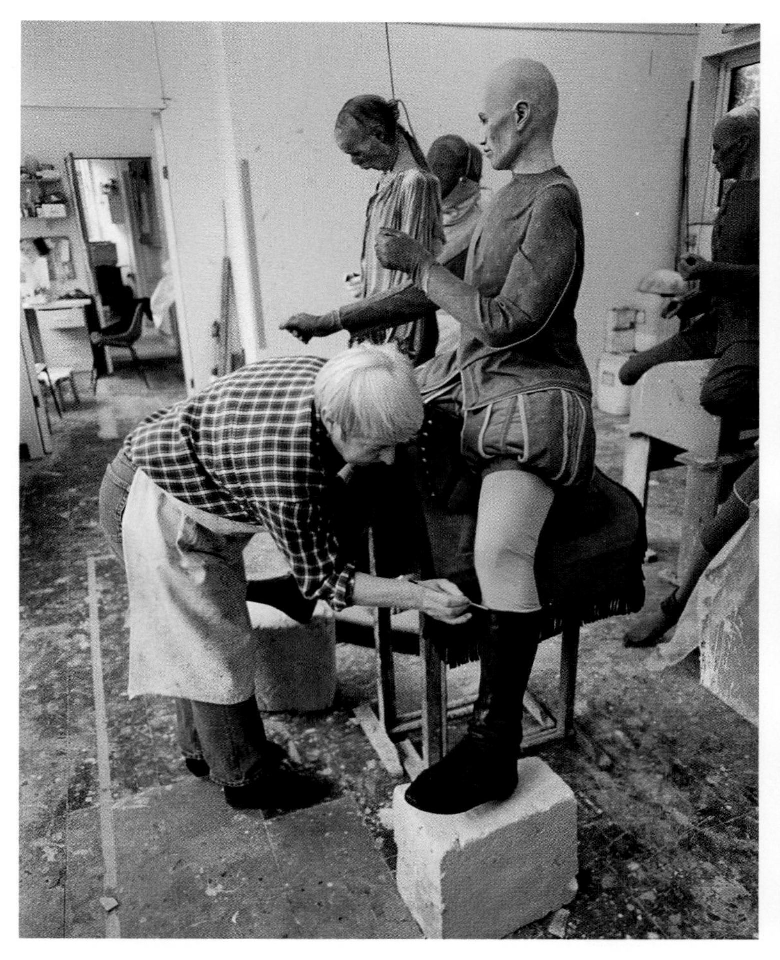

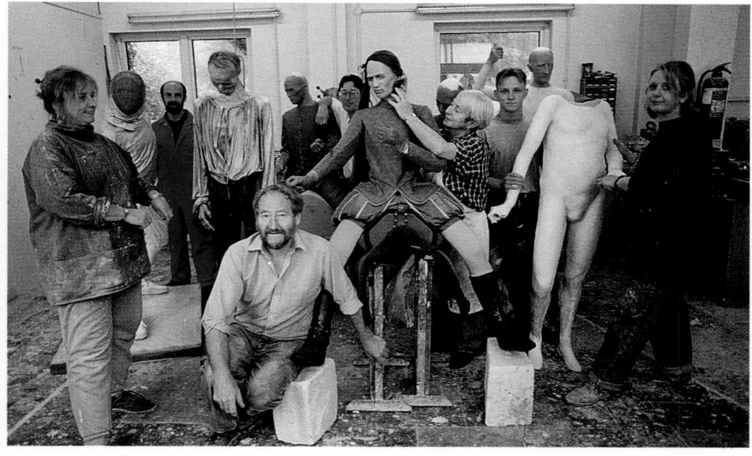

Kit Freeborn

The Freeborn studio in Cobham is strangely appropriate as a venue for the construction of material for the Royal Armouries. Prior to the Freeborn occupancy it was apparently the domain of Barnes Wallis whose pivotal role with the Dambusters rather overshadowed his extraordinary career as a scientist. Kit and his mother Jane Freeborn have a role in the project similar to that of Gerry Embleton. They sculpted all the figures for the equestrian pieces in the Oriental gallery and the mahouts for the 17th-century Indian elephant armour brought back to England in 1801. They also produced the figures for the cruciform centrepiece in the War gallery, including the figure for the magnificent Gothic armour, three additional equestrian figures, four foot soldiers and the rather sinister cadaver announcing the Self-defence gallery. The Freeborns' sculpture and immaculate sets have both wit and versatility and they take on whole environments or individual figures with equal facility.

Above: Top left and top right, the Freeborn studio; bottom right, a Berlin Café set for the Los Angeles Holocaust Museum ; left, figures in the Oriental gallery.
Opposite: Gerry Embleton's sketches for museum figures.

Films, interactives and graphics

GUY WILSON

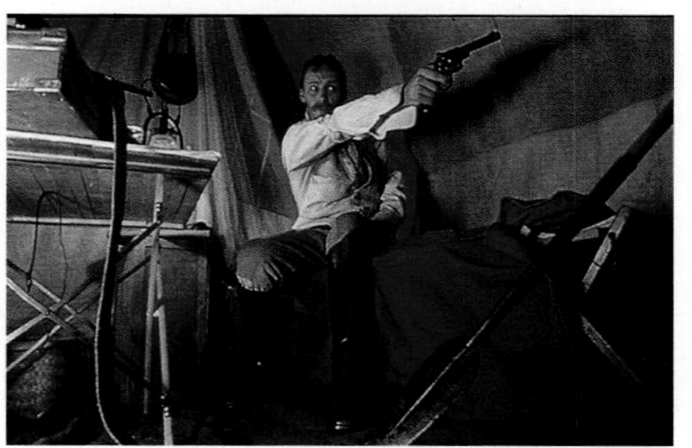

There are many things which neither static display nor live demonstration can do to explain and interpret the collections of the Royal Armouries. From its inception we intended our new museum to have a strong software base and to use film, sound, light and computers to help tell the stories which we wanted to be encompassed within the museum.

However, in planning for this we were conscious of the disadvantages as well as the advantages of reliance upon computers, which provide solitary, individual experiences, whereas research has shown clearly that most visitors to museums see a museum visit as a social, group activity, not a solitary one. This led us to develop a more 'theatrical' approach than has been common recently in museums, and we have attempted to use film and sound as far as possible to provide audience rather than individual experiences, and to limit the use of computers to areas of interpretation which only they can provide. Both for this reason and because we were determined not to experiment with the newest of technologies but to concentrate upon creative uses of well-tried techniques, electronics and machinery, we were not tempted by the latest individual experience-based developments such as virtual reality. While this may come we knew that for us its time was not yet.

We have used films to do six very different things: to tell a story (of a battle or some other event), to provide a general historical or technological background, to show how things were made, to explain how they were used and what were the consequences of their use, to introduce a particular display or gallery, and to set a mood.

To achieve this we have used a wide variety of film techniques from fully filmed reconstructions of battles, via the editing and/or compilation of existing film footage to the production of stills films using only images contemporary to the events described. The use of such a variety of film types was intentional, both because it will help prevent the museum from becoming predictable and because it will allow us to gauge the preferences of the public so that we can in time improve our use of the film medium.

The majority of these films are shown on in-gallery monitors, and therefore need to be very short. Others are screened in cinemas or smaller theatres, and these can be somewhat more leisurely. Thus the length of the films varies from three to twenty-five minutes.

In searching for such a variety of film treatments we have concentrated more upon delivering good quality results than in developing a museum style. Nevertheless some sense of style and difference has been achieved. Our maxim has become: if we can, film it ourselves. To control quality and content filming rather than editing the filming of others is very important. Where possible we have filmed dramatic events, not static pieces. Objects can best be seen in show cases, whereas films are best at showing them in action. We have avoided using to-camera presenters – they date films too quickly, and as far as possible, for similar reasons, have avoided showing people in modern dress. Finally, it will come as little surprise that we were not able to compete with feature films in the recreation of battles. To

Above: Filming for the Royal Armouries: top, *Yabusame*; bottom, *Traveller abroad.*
Opposite: The Spring Grand Festival at the Nikko Toshogu Shrine, twinned with the Royal Armouries.

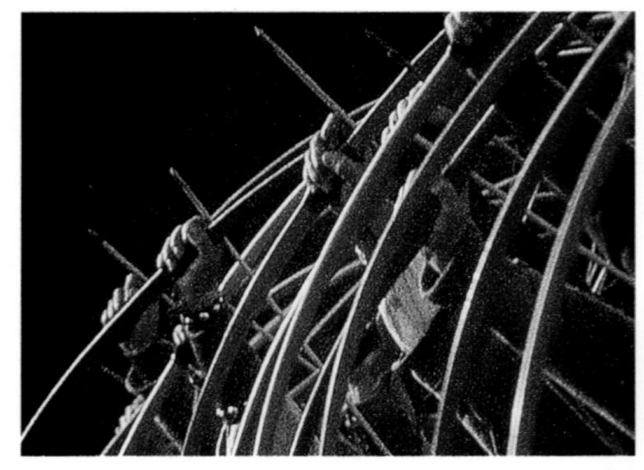

AGINCOURT

(above)

One of the two major battle reconstructions in the museum, this film tells the story of King Henry V's 1415 invasion of France and charts the course of the battle of Agincourt. The film concentrates upon the effect of the English longbows and the devastating arrow storm which they unleashed on the vast French forces.

WILD WEST

(below)

This film contrasts the myth of the West and its gun culture as we know it from the movies with the more peaceful and prosaic reality. The effect is increased by showing the movie myth in glorious Technicolor, and the reconstructed reality in grainy black and white as if it were real archive footage.

compensate for this not only did we concentrate on the details of combat – how the arms and armour was used – but we developed a rather different 'factional' style, a half-way house between feature film and historical documentary. We hope in future years to be able to continue to develop our skills in this area and expand the range of films available to the museum.

Sound on its own can be very potent. We have used it in discreet areas to give a sense of a period or a subject, to share with the public personal reminiscences and experiences from the past, and to make them aware of the real sounds of battle. We have used it in combination with lights and a tableau display to bring what to most visitors will be an obscure 16th-century Italian battle vividly to life. And in one area, the *Sound and sights of war* we have added a slide presentation and major musical extracts to the mix to give visitors an impression of the range of human responses to warfare.

All the film and sound programmes have been made for the museum by Chevron Communications, a part of Yorkshire–Tyne-Tees Television. A considerable number of directors, crews, editors and technicians have worked on this project, which for them and us meant making one film a week for almost a year. Some may have been doubtful at the beginning about working on a project to make films for a museum, but as they saw what we were about everyone involved became more and more enthusiastic and in the end gave us more of their best than we could have dared hope. The quality that has been achieved is a tribute to their enthusiasm and great skill and to the thorough organisation and artistic attention to detail of David Wilson, the Executive Producer appointed by Chris Meehan to take charge of the whole project.

In our use of computers we have been careful to restrict them to areas to which they are particularly suited, but in doing so we have again attempted to provide a very wide variety of programmes so that we can subsequently assess which are most popular and successful. Almost half of the computer terminals in the museum are in the War gallery and all these are devoted to wargaming. In the appropriate section of the gallery visitors can pit their wits on battlefields from classical times to the present century. In playing one of the games they will learn something about the tactics and weapons capability of that particular period, if they play them all they will learn about the development of tactics and weapons over the centuries. In the Hunting gallery we have developed programmes especially for younger children to help them learn how to recognise animal tracks and match animals to their correct habitats. In the Self-defence gallery the insides of weapons and how they work are revealed. In the Tournament gallery the mysteries of heraldry are humorously explained using cartoon characters, and the complexities of armour garnitures are brought home in a timed jigsaw puzzle programme. Finally, in the Oriental gallery visitors can access the museum's complete records on this part of the collection.

All these computer programmes have been developed especially for the museum by Patrick Kelly and Tony Dillon of Reflex Interactive working to briefs prepared by members of the curatorial staff under the direction of our curator of Oriental arms and armour, Thom Richardson.

Above: Filming for the Royal Armouries: top, *Yabusame*; bottom, *Traveller abroad.*

YABUSAME

(above)

Filmed on location in The Nikko Toshogu Shrine, Japan, this film explains the religious significance of *yabusame* horse archery and shows it being performed as part of the Shrine's annual Spring festival. *Yabusame* is a direct link to the skills of the horse archers of the Steppes who are so important to the story told in the Oriental gallery.

THE CAVALRY SWORD

(below)

Should a cavalry sword be made to cut, thrust or do both? This was a question which military theorists, serving soldiers and sword makers agonised over in the 19th century. This film chronicles the argument, and by showing the different swords in use graphically illustrates their power and the enormous stresses put upon them in action.

THE TRAVELLER AT HOME

(above)

Filmed on location around Leeds this film uses three scenes to explain why those travelling in England often went armed. A group of medieval travellers defend themselves against a band of brigands, a blunderbuss foils a highway robbery, and a Victorian man-about-town resorts to a sword-stick to protect his life and purse.

WILDFOWLING

(below)

Filmed on the Blackwater estuary in Essex this film both introduces the puntgunning tableau which it accompanies and shows how the massive punt guns of the professional wildfowlers and sportsmen of yesterday were loaded and used. By so doing it attempts to explain this unusual livelihood and sport.

TOURNAMENT

(above)

This film introduces the subject of the Tournament gallery to the visitors as they enter. It makes two basic points: this gallery is about sporting combat; and there are three basic types of tournament – tourney, joust and foot combat. Each of these types is briefly described and illustrated between repetitions of the two basic points.

US CIVIL WAR

(below)

Filmed on location at Cedar Creek in Pennsylvania, using members of US Civil War re-enactment societies, this film, rather than telling the story of any one battle, looks at the development and effectiveness of weapons during the US Civil War and the evolving tactics employed to take advantage of them.

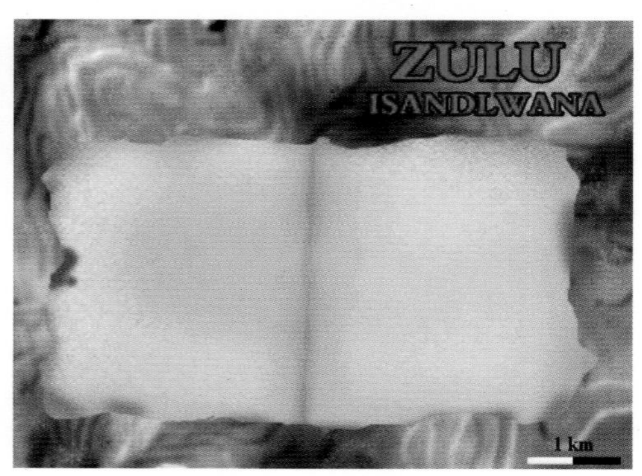

The widest variety of subjects for the interactives were chosen to test public reaction to this learning technique in an arms and armour museum. The results are both promising and amusing. It is, for instance, more fun to get some answers wrong on the Heraldry programme in the Tournament gallery than to get them right because the programme's central cartoon character has some nasty moments when the user's lack of knowledge is made apparent. Other programmes are designed specifically for younger children or for adults, and give a considerable variety of ways to learn more about arms and armour and other elements of the collection.

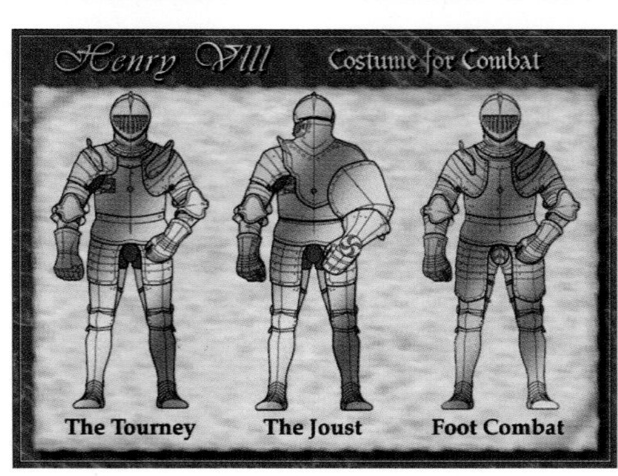

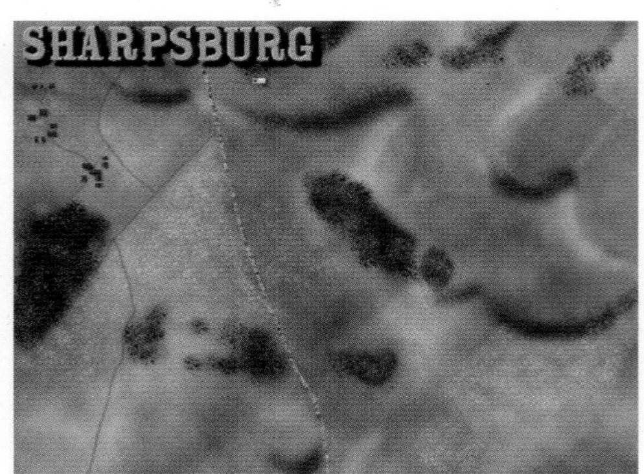

Corinthian helmet
Greek, about 600 bc
The bronze 'Corinthian' helmet is one of the most elegant forms of helmet ever made. The earliest versions appeared in Greece about 650 bc, and they were replaced by the Attic type by 500 bc.
ROYAL ARMOURIES
Islam - 751 AD

The graphic package

Words and images are vital to the coherence of a museum presentation. A thousand years of history covering all the continents of the world required organisation, intensive research and the development of a unique personal language for each gallery comprising graphic illustration, labelling, text panels, graphic and transparency walls, appropriate artwork and decorative framing. Nearly 2,000 images to illuminate the story of the objects, sourced and procured with copyright permissions by the Royal Armouries, were reproduced for display by the Works.

The location of each image, text panel and captions was digitised. When it had been sized, written and edited, each element was reproduced on a variety of surfaces, perspex, metal, composition board, canvas, gauze or timber, using computer imaging, photographic techniques, scenic painting and silk-screening.

Above: Claude Lorrain reproduction by Ric Duffield.
Left: The Works team at work in the office and workshop.
Opposite: Collage of graphics prepared for the Royal Armouries.

SELF DEFENCE
HUNTING
WAR
ROYAL ARMOURIES

Operating the Royal Armouries

EVELYN THURLBY

The appointment of a professional service organisation to operate the Royal Armouries building was a requirement of the private-sector investors, and after lengthy negotiations in December 1993 Royal Armouries International appointed Gardner Merchant. A well-established provider of contract catering services and facilities management, they came into the project with no pre-conceived ideas of how the museum should be operated.

At that time, the building had been comprehensively designed, the main contractor was nominated and a detailed budget had been established. The crucial challenge was to construct a practical operating plan which would deliver both customer satisfaction and the financial results guaranteed by the company within the envelope provided.

The first priority was to understand the building, the commercial facilities and the quality of the museum experience envisaged for the visitor. The fixed-price contract constrained our ability to make radical changes – total design integrity had to be maintained without sacrificing operating practicalities. Fortunately form and function were compatible and solutions were found that compromised neither. No area of operations were exempt from this process of close scrutiny – security, cleaning, maintenance, catering, retail, non-museum staffing, operation of the Craft Court, Menagerie, Tiltyard and shooting galleries. Also, in conjunction with Royal Armouries International and the Royal Armouries, we examined marketing, public relations and business development.

The teething troubles implicit in operating a new building and recruiting an operating team from scratch are formidable. Each element of operation has a requirement to contribute to the unique character of the museum. Retailing has to reflect the quality of the collection. Publications have to follow the graphics style developed for the museum. Catering has to take into account the varying needs of both museum visitors and corporate clients. This is achieved by providing a variety of options for the museum visitors in the coffee bars, the bistro and the Wellington restaurant. Corporate clients are offered the totality of the envelope from 20 to 600 covers in a gallery setting, the Street, or the Royal Armouries Hall, the temporary exhibition gallery, but also the largest dining room in Leeds.

To optimise use of the building, the operator has to have a positive attitude. Creative management seeks to combine the museum experiences intended for the visitor with the variety of corporate and community uses for which the building was also designed.

A flexible approach means that operations can respect the basic requirements of a national museum, *gravitas*, quality, security, climatic control, good housekeeping and design rigour, and make the project commercially successful. It is up to operations to make the visitor experience pleasurable, informative and welcoming and to deliver a sensitive management approach in the public areas. The focus and inspiration at all times in our staff development is this need to serve the visitor and to make the collection truly accessible.

Above: From top to bottom: dining in the Edwardian gun room; the Nelson bistro; the Wellington restaurant; easy access throughout for the handicapped.
Opposite: The Street at night.

Conclusion

SIR JAMES GLOVER

In early 1993 the ambitious plan for a splendid new Royal Armouries in Leeds had reached an impasse. Without a private sector partner the project would founder. Thus it happened that I was asked by the country's leading venture-capitalist (3i) to examine the commercial possibilities of forming a plc to build, run and subsequently develop the museum. Together with Christopher O'Boyle (Chief Executive), we drew up a business plan to attract the much-needed private investment.

Initially, the role of the private sector, embodied in the plc, was to ensure that the vision of the Royal Armouries Trustees, so ably executed by the Master, was translated into reality. We raised the private investment and created a financial infrastructure, carried the responsibility for constructing the museum and provided the framework for the displays. We now, with the dedicated support of the curatorial staff, intend to deliver not only an exciting visitor experience but one which is commercially successful.

We inherited the product of literally years of detailed research and planning undertaken by the Trustees and their advisors. It was of the very highest order. Within it lay the contribution of the City of Leeds and its Development Corporation, solid evidence of their enthusiasm for the project. Special mention must be made of the professionalism and flair of the architect, Derek Walker, whose influence pervades all. But it is the partnership forged between the staffs of the Royal Armouries and the plc which is the key. The path has not been easy. What is artistically desirable is not always commercially achievable, and vice versa. Yet our fortunes and aspirations are inextricably entwined. We will share every success, and any failure too. This has produced a fine team spirit with remarkable levels of co-operation, and indeed understanding.

Many disciplines, each with their own agendas and interests, have been welded together to create the framework for the museum. There is the consortium of blue chip investors headed by 3i with Electra Investment Trust, Yorkshire Electricity and Gardner Merchant as partners. It is they, and not the public sector, who carry the financial risks. Alfred McAlpine have brought the breadth of their experience to deliver the building on time and within budget. Our landlords, the British Waterways Board, provide another dimension and are our joint venture partners in developing the site and its water surroundings. The intricate role of project manager has been admirably fulfilled by Heery's International. The contributions of a myriad of contractors ranging from the brick manufacturers to animal-modelmakers and restaurant specialists have been programmed into the project. Gardner Merchant, in a different capacity, play a critical part as the operator co-ordinating all aspects of the day to day running of the museum.

In sum the new Royal Armouries represents a celebration of public and private sector co-operation. Innovation, excellence and interactivity are the guiding principles. They combine to present a museum of which Leeds, and indeed the nation, can be justly proud.

Above: Sir James Glover
Left: The opening of the museum by Her Majesty the Queen and the presentation of the royal masque, 15 March 1996.

The Project Team

ROYAL ARMOURIES

Trustees

Royal Armouries Personnel

Guy Wilson
Peter Hammond

Curatorial

Ian Eaves, Thom Richardson, Graeme Rimer

Vaughan Allen, David Bryant, Bridget Clifford, Chris Gravett, Nick Hall, Chris Henry
Angus Konstam, Philip Lankester, Mark Murray-Flutter, Martin Pegler, Peter Smithurst, Karen Watts
Fred Wilkinson

Live Interpretation

John Waller

Education

Chris Scott

Irene Davies, Mark Folwell, Andrea Sinclair, Ann Todd, Mary Walsh, Annabel Wigner

Library

Philip Abbott, Sarah Barter-Bailey, Jane Hall, Sharon Tibbots

Registrars

David Beck, David Blackmore, Andrew Bodley, Robert Chester, Robert Crosby, Andrew Deane
Keith Ducklin, Tinuke Otoki, Sharon Scarmazzo, Sadi Sengel

Conservation

Robert Smith

Dave Bull, Alison Draper, Edward Dunn, Ronnie Gibbs, Andrew Gordon, Alison Guppy
Nathan Jones, Colin Lindley, Toby McNicol, Roy Mandeville, Chris Smith, Robert Sneddon
Kate Stockwell, Donna Stevens, Richard West, Susie Wright

Publications, Design and Photography

Jeremy Hall, John Penna, Alastair Pether, Paula Turner, Bob Wheller

Marketing and Development

Dick Mundell

Nick Boole, Samantha Bramwell, Sian Lewis, Cathy McDermott, Tanya Ronn, Henrietta Usherwood
Rosemary Watters

Finance and Administration

Derek Croucher

Barbara Anderson, Helen Biggin, Brendan Davies, Joanna Donkin, Denise Ferry, Julie Framp
Tim Green, Meneasa Murphy, Carol Moon, Tony Reddin, Mark Roffey, Lyn Stone

Security

David Harris

Personnel

Jan Bruce, Liz Cridland, Debrorah Tarrant

ROYAL ARMOURIES MUSEUM CONSULTANTS

Derek Walker Associates - Architects, Planners & Display Designers

Planning of Clarence Dock

Derek Walker, Julian Baker, Michael Brett, Julian Cowie, Markus Geiger, David Reddick
Neil Southard, Tomo Utsumi

Building

Derek Walker, Julian Baker, Keith Barrell, Douglas Benneworth, Neil Miller-Chalk, David Reddick
Aaron McCaffrey, Balvinder Obhi, Markus Geiger, Michael Ridden

Display

Derek Walker, Julian Baker, John Bury, Elizabeth Bury, Neil Miller-Chalk, David Reddick
Aaron McCaffrey, Michael Ridden, Neil Southard, Tomo Utsumi, Jan Walker, John Wright

Landscaping

Neil Higson, Tony Southard

Graphics

Brian Tattersfield, Mary Tattersfield, Jane Tattersfield, Paul Astbury, Gillian Hodgson, Nigel James MacFall

Lighting

Phillip Reddiough – Museum & Gallery Lighting Ltd

Royal Armouries Museum Identity

Minale, Tattersfield & Partners Ltd

Heery – Project Mangement

Michael J Clayton, Christopher J Cormie, Simon R Davis, Paul Hill, Jeffrey Taylor

Buro Happold – Structural, Mechanical & Electrical Engineers

Sir Edmund Happold, Rod Macdonald

Dave Beck, Peter Brooke, Terry Ealey, Simon Ford, Vincent Grant, Mick Green
Steve Gregson, Mike Hall, Alan Harbinson, Mike Harrison, Tristram Hope, David Hull
David Kingstone, Peter Moseley, Teresa Murphy, Adrian Pottinger, Tom Skalles, Roger Spurr
Simon Wainwright, Rodger Webster, Jenny Wheelwright, Neil Wright

Rex Procter & Partners – Quantity Surveyors

Ian Armitage

Stephen Norman, Philip Rushbrook, Ian Tomlinson, Craig Dransfield, Eric Ginn, Andy Halls
Chris Pearcey, Ken Bromley, Frank Whiteley, Tony Chaplin, George Baran, Carol Foster
Maxine Lofthouse, Hazel Rennison, Kath Newton

YTV – Films & Audio-visual

Mike Harris, Chris Meehan, David Wilson

Daniel Hoffman, Gary Lunn, David James, Melanie Davis, Amanda Chary, Serena Kennedy
Amanda Clegg, Alan Bell, Mike Cocker, Tony Scull, Rick Vanes, Tony Males

Royal Armouries Marketing and Public Relations Consultants

Hill & Knowlton (UK) Ltd – Public Relations
James Cooke
Zita Adamson, Tony Whiting

Barrington Johnson Lorains – Advertising Agency

Brian Allan, Ian Banner, Andy Cartin, Steve Carolan, Stuart Dally, Dave Forster
Anne-Marie Glennon, Sarah Hardcastle, Steve Johnson, Marcus Leigh, Trevor Lorains, Michael Murray
Jane Stafford, Claire Stewardson

Ptarmigan Consultants – Public Relations Agency

Niyi Akeju, Graham Barnes, Gordon Forbes, Jane Hunt, Kathy McLaughlin

DTZ Debenham Thorpe – Surveyors

Judith Atkinson

Hammond Studdards – Solicitors

Simon Inman, Patrick Mitchell, Ian Chuttleworth

Pinsent Curtis – Solicitors

Stephen Chandler, Mark Hill, Nigel McClea, John Richie, Richard Penfold, Jeremy Summers
Frank Suttie

Schroders – Financial Consultants

Richard Beales, George Wadia

DEPARTMENT OF NATIONAL HERITAGE

Dr Kenneth Gray, Chris Atkins, David Chesterton, Paul Douglas, Mike Keatinge, Andrew Robson
Gerard Wheeldon

LEEDS CITY COUNCIL

Cllr Jon Trickett

Brian Walker, BP Atha, D Atkinson, A Carter, K Loudon, K Parker
E Minkin

Officers

E J S Anderson, J D Ansbro, P Brook, K Brown, R Buchan, I Butterworth
C Follin, S Hacker, R Howell, A Knowles, A Shelton, J Siddall
K Siddall, M Turnbull, S Speak, P Toner, J D Wallis

LEEDS DEVELOPMENT CORPORATION

Peter Hartley

Martin Eagland   Alan Goodrum   Robin Herzberg   Stuart Kenny   Nigel Tipple   Robert Wolfe

BRITISH WATERWAYS

David Ingman   Bernard Henderson

Richard Curtis   Mike Finkill   David Fisher   Jeremy Harrison   Jayne Holland   Ian Valder

Ian White

LEEDS & BRADFORD CHAMBER OF COMMERCE

John Jackson   Peter Coles-Johnson   Tony Grant   Edward Holdroyd   David Richardson   Arnold Ziff

ROYAL ARMOURIES (INTERNATIONAL) PLC

Sir James Glover

Christopher O'Boyle   Michael Herbert   David K Wilkinson

Sally-Anne Bennett   Caroline Driver   Susan Dykes   Len Entwistle   Lynne Hardwick   Elizabeth Harmer
Martin Lock   Mavis Marshall   Jacqueline Pelter   Julian Rawel   John Rodger   Pauline Sheridan
Brian Stemmings   Patricia Sykes

Investors Board

Bank of Scotland

Raymond Clark   T O Hutchinson   W G McQueen   Austin T Reilly   David Spencer

3i plc

Patrick Dunne   Martin Gagen   Ian Lobley   Ewen Mcpherson   Clive Moody   Jonathan Russell
David K Wilkinson

Gardner Merchant Ltd

Garry Hawkes

Ian Carslaw   Nick Drabble   David King   Maurice McBride   Charles McCole   Stephen McManus

Scarcroft Investments Ltd

Malcolm Chatwin   Roger Dickinson   Christopher Hampson

Electra Group

Marc Boughton   Oliver J H Huntsman   Michael Stoddard

Gardner Merchant Leisure Services, Facilities Management & IT Department

Lynda Brennan   Alan Brockington   Comley Hamilton   Simon Jefford   Owen Johnson   David King
Bob Lonsdale   Stephen McManus   John Murphey   John Pitts   Georgette Rouse   Evelyn Thurlby
Thomas Toland

Safegard – Environmental Services

John Dyson   Nick Warwick

Lockharts – Kitchen Design

John Fitzgibbon   Rob Hand   Gary Hodgson

Edinburgh Consultancy – Retail

Dibb Lupton Broomhead – Solicitors

Hunslet Employment Services – Recruitment

Bradford University Management Centre – Best Practice Management

Gardner Merchant Ltd – Operators

Elaine Noble

Peter Agnew   Martin Barratt   John Braithwaite   Lynda Brennan   Clinton Brookes   Mike Brooksbank
Sarah Burbridge   David Burgoyne   Pat Casey   Annette Crowther   Darren Dunwell   Simon Evans
Darren Foden   Wayne Foster   Colin Gott   John Hayley   Deborah Hickinson   Maureen Holburt
Marian Jones   Chris Jennings   Victoria Johnson   Martin Lock   Tracey McMaster   Sarah Millington
Catherine Morgan   Dave Penny   Richard Powell   Rachel Puttick   Jeanette Ramsden   Gloria Rawle
Georgette Rouse   Carol Ann Wadeley   Susan Wadlow   Chris Warden   Paul Whitlock

Interpreters

John Berry   Andrew Bodley   Craig Cowdrouy   Henry Clayton   Anne Caulfield   Andrew Deane
Keith Ducklin   Alan Eyles   Adam des Forges   Stuart Greig   Sally Hague   Frank Hammond
Dominic Magentey   Kate Marshall   Dominic Pickard   Geoffrey Pye   Rebecca Sparnon   John Thompson
Michala Watson   John White

Lakeland Bird of Prey Centre

James Buttle   Karen Gray   Chris Stimpson

Craftsmen

Mark Beaby   Peter Dyson   Chris Dobson

Defenco – Security

Gordon Elliott   Steve Jones   Saffron Palmer   Adrian Payne

BUILDING CONTRACT

Alfred McAlpine – Main Contractor

Martin Whiteley – Senior Project Manager

David Alcock, Richard Baldwin, Brian Benson, Alistair Bewley, Nick Cable, Julian Carr, Phil Cartwright, Richard Cave, John Colley, Henry Curtis, John Colley, Steve Darlington, Paul Durston, Bob Dutton, Jerry Ellis, Craig Foster, Alan Gardner, John Goldsbrough, Eric Gilbert, Gary Grennan, Dawn Hick, Paul Hunter, Peter Kendal, Tony Lee, Luke Makin, Ray Moore, Stuart Place, Brian Pringle, John Quayle, Andrew Rose, Tommy Sands, Melvyn Schless, Ian Whalley, Steve Williams, Beryl Wilson, Tom Wilson

Mark Witherington

Leach Rhodes & Walker – Architects to McAlpines

Jeff Varnom, David Baxter, Rodney Kay, Jeff Whillance, John Bradley

Deacon Callard – Structural Engineers to McAlpines

Colin Cheetham, Mike Bailey, Richard Blake, Bill Catlow, Steve Douglas, David Else, Bert Greenhalgh, Karl Hill, John Holden, Jim Holland, Colin Laxton, Ray Leech

Theresa Murphy, Alan Parkinson, Jack Pilkington, John Thomas, Graham Watson

Hadens – Mechanical & Electrical Contractors

Dennis Whitley

Stuart Driscol, Trevor Espie, Jim Eyre, Colin Finlay, Ian Green, John Hayley, Dave Longsdale, Mark Martindale, Terry Pass, Alan Smith, Rob Speakman, Simon Turner

Alfred McAlpine Subcontractors

Subcontractor	Work
A Andrews & Son Ltd	*Natural stone cladding & floors*
AV Technology Ltd	*Accoustic consultants*
Alderburgh Ltd	*Methane membrane*
Allbuild Supplies Ltd	*Inner leaf blocks*
Architen Ltd	*Canvas roofs*
Barflo-Lca	*External mains*
Beeley Fabrication Ltd	*Miscellaneous steelwork*
Brooke Edgeley Specialist Technical Services Ltd	*Lighting protection*
British Waterways Board	*Flood defence gates*
CD and Company	*Floor & wall tiles*
Cannock Chase Concrete	*Miscellaneous precast concrete*
Cawood Dixon Ltd	*Ceramic floors & walls*
Contest Melbourne Ltd	*Concrete testing*
County Forge Ltd	*Balustrades*
Coxdome Ltd	*Rooflights*
Cuerden Timber & Joinery	*Joinery & doors*
Edwin Dyson & Sons Ltd	*Timber balustrades*
End Systems Ltd	*Commissioning*
Erco	*Gallery lighting*
Exploration Associates	*Pile probing*
Fire Check Systems Ltd	*Fire protection*
Framford Kitchens	*Kitchen units*
Frederick Jones & Son	*Recessed manhole & drawpit covers*
Glencroft Civil Eng Ltd	*Substructure & drainage*
Hewetson Floors Ltd	*Raised floors*
Hollicourt Ltd	*Miscellaneous steelwork*
IPS Ltd	*Roof membrane*
IES Water Softness of Water Treatment Ltd	*Water treatment*
John Abbott Ltd	*Flexible floors*
John Atkinson Ltd	*GRG cove*
Koltek Ltd	*Window cleaning equipment*
Lainton Services Ltd	*Methane membrane*
Lee Sanitation Ltd	*Miscellaneous river works*
M J Hester Plasterers	*Plastering*
Malcolm Hughes	*Compliance survey*
Millbank Electronics Ltd	*PA system*
New Vent Distributors Ltd	*Flues*
Parkman Building Engineer	*Lock gate consultants*
Perkin Bros	*Plastering*
Phoenix Landscapes Ltd	*Soft landscaping*
ABS Pumps Ltd	*Submersible pumps*
A Proctor Developments	*Concrete ancillaries*
Alfred Bagnell & Sons	*Painting & decoration*
Amber Doors Ltd	*Internal metal sliding doors*
Baggeridge	*Bricks*
BBC Fire Protection Ltd	*Fire detection systems*
Beldan (UK) Ltd	*Folding doors*
British Gas Plc	*Gas*
British Telecom	*Telecommunications*
Broxap & Corby Ltd	*Street furniture*
C J Watker	*Mastic joint sealing*
Cape Ceilings Ltd	*Suspended ceiling & tiles*
Concord	*Museum and Street lighting*
Cooper Rigg Ltd	*Metal balustrades*
Cowill Construction Ltd	*Metal stud partitions & sus. ceilings*
Crittal Windows Ltd	*Craft Court glazing*
Durabella Ltd	*Hardwood floors*
Encon Insulation Ltd	*Insulation*
E Rushworth Ltd	*Ventilation ductwork*
Expanded Piling Company	*Piling*
Faltec Doors Ltd	*External sliding folding doors*
Firth Carpets Ltd	*Carpets*
Frank Graham Consult Engs	*Consultant*
G Sanders	*Masonry contractor*
Greenwood Airvac	*Metal louvres*
Hodkin & Jones Ltd	*GRG & GRP products*
Inglecrag Insulation Co Ltd	*Thermal insulation*
IMS Building Products Ltd	*Roof drainage*
J W Taylor	*Suspended ceilings*
John Alderson	*Asbestos removal*
Ken Moorhead Excavation Ltd	*Demolition*
L J Church Laboratory Ltd	*Soil testing*
Leeds Design Consultancy	*Asbestos removal*
Lewes Design Consult. Ltd	*Hall of Steel stairs*
Menvier-Amberlec Systems Ltd	*Emergency lighting*
Marconi Security Systems	*Electronic security*
Northern Doors Co Ltd	*Roller shutters*
P&W Site Fixing	*General structural steel*
Pendant Aluminium Ltd	*Glass ceilings*
Petbow Generators UK	*Emergency generator*
Pilkington Architectural	*Planar glazing*

Polstore Ltd	*Polstore racks*	Process Heat Ltd	*Trace heating*
Preussag Fire Protection Ltd	*Dry risers*	Robertson Vogue Ltd	*Ventilators*
Redsure Gas Products Ltd	*Special gases*	Roger Bullivant	*Lock operators cabin piling*
S Marshall & Son Ltd	*Paving blocks & kerbs*	SCC Ltd	*RC superstructure*
Schindler Ltd	*Lifts*	Schuco	*Glazing systems*
Sheffield Insulation Ltd	*Insulation*	Solaglas Ltd	*Internal glazing*
Staefa Control Systems Ltd	*BMS controls*	Spel Products Ltd	*Drainage interceptor*
Spiral Staircase Systems	*Spiral stair*	Sportsmac	*Performance turf*
Sports Maintenance Ltd	*Tiltyard reinforced turf*	Steve Poole	*Tiled roofs*
Style Life Windows	*Glazing*	Tarmac Masonry Ltd	*Reconstituted stone*
Taylor Maxwell & Co Ltd	*Facing bricks*	Teesdale Surfacing Ltd	*Hard landscaping*
Tilcon Mortar Ltd	*Mortar*	Tilcon Surfacing Ltd	*Surfacing*
Triple Engineering Ltd	*Miscellaneous steelwork*	WestYorks Waste Tech GRP	*Gas monitoring*
Westbury Tubular Ltd	*Structural SS & planar glazing*	Wincro Metal Industries	*Masonry fixings*
W M Reid Engineering Ltd	*Pontoon*	Yorkshire Demolitions	*Tank removal*
Yorkshire Electricity	*Electricity*	Yorkshire Water Services	*Water*

DISPLAY CONTRACT

Andy Thornton – Gallery Fitout

Chris Wilcock

Eammon Cassidy   David Hurst   Richard Johnson   John Pearcy   Pat Stewart   Richard Woods

A Andrews & Sons Ltd	*Slate cladding*	Hodkin & Jones Ltd	*GRG, GRP & fibrous plaster*
Metalwork Ltd	*Structural steelwork*	Stanley Walker & Son Ltd	*Partitions*
Wheelhouse & Noble Ltd	*Electrical installation*	Wendy Wall	*Sculptor and Artist*

Goppion – Museum Showcases

Sandro Goppion

Mauro Bandelli   Giacomo Borace   Isa Ferioli   Romano Gerelli   Piero Pagani

Click – Museum Showcases

James Webster   Andrew Clarke   Helen Oates

Gibson Lea Ltd	*Timber panels*	Plumb Group	*Timber panels*
Romag Security Laminators Ltd	*Glass*	Scott and Bailey Sheetmetal Co.	*Steelwork & sheet metal work*
Solaglas Ltd	*Glass*		

The Works – Graphics

Dave Gledhill   Roy Webber   Karen Webber

Ric Duffield   William Gaunt   Dean Houseman   Ben Jamieson   Barry Menzer   Paul Peppiate

Kevin Spark   Ben Webber   Lee Webber   Robert Wright

Warrens Imaging – Large photographic reproductions, mounting & laminating and photoCD scans

Gordon Models – Architectural Models, Sets & Structures

Bill Gordon   Brian Archer   Philip Moulton   Christopher Rutherford

Philip Allen	*Mail*	Karen Borne	*Knight & horse tunics*
Perry Braham	*Mechanical design*	Barry Dodd	*Electronics*
Maurice DeBroise	*Engineering*	Tony Harris	*Armour*
Derek Howarth	*Sculptor*	Dave Johnson	*Joinery*
Bill Johnson	*Stainless steel*	Su Lawrence	*Artist*
Melanie Reynolds	*Artist*	Adrian Marchant Studio	*Fibreglass*
Bill Walsh	*Uxbridge glass*	John Waterhouse	*Tent maker*
Dee Waterhouse	*Tent maker*	Mary Waterhouse	*Tent maker*

David Hayes – Animal Sculptures

David Hayes   Mikki Labangudgeirsdottir   Stuart Delaney   Philip Szanislo   David Pickles

Freeborns – Sets and Figures

Kit Freeborn   Patricia Freeborn   Tamsin Evans   Tom Joynson

Time Machine AG – Sets and Figures

Gerry Embleton   Keith Bartlett   Françoise Bolli   Anne Embleton   Sophie Embleton   Monique Flood

William Hutt   Angela Lowes

AVE – Audio Visual Equipment

Simon Harris   Simon Banks   Steve Chapman   Tom Coucher   Sarah Gorman   David James

Richard Leslie   Steve Ockendon   Richard Studerus

Reflex Interactive – Computer Interactives

Patrick Kelly   Mark Alleyne   Matthew Baxter   Chris Clark   Anthony Dillon   Jon Haines

Chris Keir   Anthony Lawrence   Edwin Mullen   Wilson Sharp   Paul Stapley   Michael Sutin

H & H Sculptors – Horses

Christopher Gomm   Caroline Morgan   Paul Wilkinson   Dante Arrigucci   Craig Westlake